TEACHING
from the
HEART
of
MINDFULNESS

VERMONT COLLEGE OF FINE ARTS
LIBRARY
36 COLLEGE STREET
MONTPELIER, VT 05602

D1295120

TEACHING

from the

HEART

of

MINDFULNESS

LAUREN ALDERFER

Foreword by
His Holiness The XIV Dalai Lama

Preface by
Meena Srinivasan

GREEN WRITERS PRESS   *Brattleboro, Vermont*

© 2015 by Lauren Alderfer
All rights reserved. No part of this book may be reproduced in any form or by any means, electronic or mechanical, including photocopying, recording, or by any information storage and retrieval system, without permission in writing from the publisher.

Printed in the United States

10 9 8 7 6 5 4 3 2 1

Green Writers Press is a Vermont-based publisher whose mission is to spread a message of hope and renewal through the words and images we publish. Throughout we will adhere to our commitment to preserving and protecting the natural resources of the earth. To that end, a percentage of our proceeds will be donated to environmental activist groups like 350.org. Green Writers Press gratefully acknowledges support from individual donors, friends, and readers to help support the environment and our publishing initiative.

GReen
wriTers
press

Giving Voice to Writers & Artists Who Will Make the World a Better Place
Green Writers Press | Brattleboro, Vermont
www.greenwriterspress.com

Parts of this book have been used with permission from *Teaching as a Spiritual Practice,* 2008, Lauren Alderfer, Full Circle Publishing, New Delhi.

The Tibetan symbols and motifs were used with permission from *The Encyclopedia of Tibetan Symbols and Motifs,* 1999, Robert Beer, Shambhala Publications, Boston, Massachusetts.

For free audio recordings of mindfulness practices from this book, teacher resources, classroom posters, inspirational cards, and much more, visit: www.laurenalderfer.com

LIBRARY OF CONGRESS CONTROL NUMBER: 2015938902
ISBN: 978-0-9960872-7-8

PRINTED ON PAPER WITH PULP THAT COMES FROM FSC-CERTIFIED FORESTS, MANAGED FORESTS THAT GUARANTEE RESPONSIBLE ENVIRONMENTAL, SOCIAL, AND ECONOMIC PRACTICES BY LIGHTNING SOURCE ALL WOOD PRODUCT COMPONENTS USED IN BLACK & WHITE, STANDARD COLOR, OR SELECT COLOR PAPERBACK BOOKS, UTILIZING EITHER CREAM OR WHITE BOOKBLOCK PAPER, THAT ARE MANUFACTURED IN THE LAVERGNE, TENNESSEE PRODUCTION CENTER ARE SUSTAINABLE FORESTRY INITIATIVE® (SFI®) CERTIFIED SOURCING

To all my teachers, past, present, and future

CONTENTS

 *A Mindful Journey*

Appendix

FOREWORD

A S HUMAN BEINGS WE ALL WANT to live a happy life, but we need a realistic method to achieve our goal. These days, in our materialistic culture, many people are led to believe that money is the ultimate source of happiness. Consequently, when they don't have enough, they feel let down. Therefore, it is important to let people know that they have the source of contentment and happiness within themselves, and that it is related to nurturing our natural inner values.

In this book, *Teaching from the Heart of Mindfulness*, Lauren Alderfer explains how it is possible to cultivate warmheartedness through the practice of mindfulness. She outlines how we can nourish our basic human nature and become happier individuals. Scientists are increasingly finding evidence that warmheartedness is essential to our general well-being and is something we are equipped with from infancy. It yields a calm mind and self-confidence, which means we can act openly, honestly, and transparently, free from anxiety, fear, and suspicion. It is the basis not only for becoming happier ourselves, but for creating a happier, more peaceful world. It is something I myself find useful and I recommend readers try it for themselves.

November 24, 2014

HIS HOLINESS THE XIV DALAI LAMA

PREFACE

TEACHING IS A SACRED TASK. As educators we are dedicated to making the world a better place, and mindfulness is a powerful means to that end. Mindfulness is the practice we engage in. It's a kind, curious, and compassionate awareness that we bring to the present moment.

Dr. Lauren Alderfer is a pioneer in the field of mindfulness in education. Well before the term "mindfulness" had entered the mainstream, she had thoughtfully embedded mindfulness into her teaching practice, classroom instruction, and teacher-education work. I had the gift of working with her when she taught at the American Embassy School (AES) in New Delhi, India. During one of my first weeks at AES, I had the privilege of attending a professional development workshop that she facilitated based on one of her earlier books, *Teaching as a Spiritual Practice: Cultivating*

Ethical Values for Self-Renewal and Transformation. I was deeply inspired by the depth of reflection she brought forth through both her writing and her warm, loving presence.

That same depth, warmth, and love radiate through the pages of this book, *Teaching from the Heart of Mindfulness.* Every page invites educators to cultivate their inner lives in the daily act of teaching while developing mindfulness and compassion. With many mindfulness-based curricula being implemented these days, Lauren's book fills an important gap in truly supporting the development of personal practice for teachers. After providing a thorough grounding in mindfulness, Lauren takes us on a journey through key aspects of mindfulness practice, from courage to compassion to perseverance. Each chapter includes a guided meditation followed by a vivid classroom application of the practice. Lauren also provides us with very useful tools like the HEARTS Mindfulness-Based Teaching Approach, BREATH, and Mindful Prayer Flags to help embed the practice of mindfulness into our teaching lives.

An authentic voice, coming from years of personal mindfulness practice and experience, is palpable in every word of this inspiring book, which makes it the perfect complement for any mindfulness-based classroom curriculum. *Teaching from the Heart of*

Mindfulness emphasizes mindfulness as a way of *being* rather than *doing*. It is this "heartfulness"[1] that teachers then transmit to their students. Lauren's Mindfulness-Based Teaching Approach not only provides the necessary tools and resources to shift pedagogy, but it is also easily adaptable for students to practice.

Students are reflections of their teachers, and as teachers, the most important teachings we offer transcend academic skills and the acquisition of knowledge. Before teaching content, we must create a learning environment conducive for education. This book is a beautiful guide to help educators cultivate an inner sense of love, so they can receive students with warmth and create a classroom filled with peace.

Teaching from the Heart of Mindfulness shows us what a truly mindful teaching practice looks like. From her own depth of practice, Lauren courageously shares examples of her classroom experiences that will inspire teachers new to mindfulness as well as seasoned practitioners. She is a teachers' teacher, and her reflective, compassionate voice communicates wisdom with kindness and grace.

MEENA SRINIVASAN
Author of *Teach, Breathe, Learn: Mindfulness In and Out of the Classroom*

---

[1] The Sanskrit root *cit* refers to the mind, consciousness, and heart, and it is the author's understanding that an experience of mindfulness is one that occurs with a deep connection of heart. In several languages, the word for mind and heart are the same.

INTRODUCTION

*A hallmark of mindfulness is the silencing
of the mind, giving way to the expanding
expression of the heart in the all-knowing
present moment. In that stillness there
emerges a sacred connection to all.*

*T*eaching from the Heart of Mindfulness
approaches teaching as a laboratory for practicing mindfulness as a way of being—from
the heart, in presence, and as a teacher. These pages
cultivate this quieting of the mind, which, in turn,
gives way to the expanding expression of the heart
in the all-knowing present moment. This presence of
being, where a sense of peace and well-being emerge,
where a deep sense of wholeness dwells, where compassion spreads its light, is at the heart of mindfulness.

Nourishing these qualities, the seeds of mindfulness, while in the very act of teaching, find their expression through the mindfulness-based teaching approach exemplified throughout the book. This approach invites teachers into a warmhearted open presence of being, grounded in a growing heartfelt calm-abiding, so that teaching from the heart of mindfulness can take firm root.

Above all, mindfulness is heart-centered, and *Teaching from the Heart of Mindfulness* invites teachers into its warmhearted nature. As a cadre of mindful teachers enters classrooms, professional development that nourishes this heartfelt quality contributes to the growing field of mindfulness in education. Interestingly, *heartfulness* is an emerging term and may more accurately describe the concept of mindfulness within a framework of Western thought. This might be, in part, because in the West wisdom is thought of as being in the mind, which is considered to be in the head. On the Asian subcontinent, where I have lived and taught most of the past twenty years, the seat of wisdom is considered to be in the heart rather than the head. *Anahata*—literally, "unstuck"—is the Sanskrit word describing the energy of the heart. For at the very heart of our day-to-day lives, including typical teaching days, beyond limiting thoughts and emotions of the mind or intellect and unbound by time or space, there is an inner dwelling of the heart, a place stemming from a deep peace and all-knowing. Therein lies an openness of receiving and growing in love, a spaciousness of heart and mind that is always unstuck, always whole. The practice of mindfulness cultivates this unfolding process. By teaching from the heart of mindfulness, teachers—and, by direct consequence, their students—are welcomed into this spaciousness of heart.

If all of life is viewed as a laboratory for practicing mindfulness, then mindfulness can unfold as a way of being in both the personal and professional arenas. To translate this guiding belief as a mindfulness-based teaching approach became my challenge. Over time I did so by developing a concrete, step-by-step process, explained in greater detail later in the book. It links the personal cultivation of mindfulness and the daily teaching experience, inviting teachers to experience mindfulness as a way of being more and more in their own lives, including their teaching lives.

Another key component is that this mindfulness-based teaching approach views mindfulness not as something to be done in a classroom as a skill as much as it is a belief and paradigm with which to approach teaching and learning. While complementing social and emotional learning and mindfulness as a skill, a mindfulness-based teaching approach is not done in fifteen-minute, deliverable chunks; instead, it can be integrated into classroom teaching strategies and student learning outcomes in any subject area. This kind of approach supports a mindful way of thinking and being throughout the teaching day and beyond, one that can be adapted to any curriculum, student population, teaching context, or school setting.

The word *mindfulness* was rarely used and little understood in the field of education when my journey developing a mindfulness-based teaching approach began. Since then, mindfulness has quietly yet powerfully entered into our daily lexicon: in education, parenting, health fields, TED Talks, and the business arena. With the exciting synergy between East and West occurring in the area of mindfulness, insights into the understanding of the word mindfulness may be useful. In Eastern religious traditions, mindfulness has deep roots, going all the way back to the centuries-old practice of monks meditating in caves throughout the Himalayas. However, it was not until 1987 that some of the first dialogues between Eastern practitioners and Western scientists were initiated, such as those organized by Tenzin Gyatso, the Fourteenth Dalai Lama, through the Mind and Life Institute. In the West, researchers, scientists, neurobiologists, and others are now quantifying functions of the brain to explain the benefits of mindfulness practice. The pioneering research of Richard J. Davidson has demonstrated potential effects of mindfulness by studying expert meditators; his recent studies reveal change to the actual makeup of their genes. Thanks to many such scientific studies, the positive impact of mindfulness on academic, social, and emotional learning is now a matter of established fact.

The translation of the Pali word *sati* includes "mindfulness," "concentrated attention," "inspection," "reflective awareness," and "retention." Jon Kabat-Zinn, the creator of the Mindfulness-Based Stress Reduction (MBSR) program, who is considered the father of mindfulness in North America, provides this operational definition of *mindfulness*: "The awareness that arises through paying attention on purpose in the present moment and non-judgmentally, to the unfolding of experience moment to moment." Thich Nhat Hanh, the world-famous Vietnamese Zen Buddhist monk, who is revered for embodying mindfulness, writes that "mindfulness is to become completely alive and live deeply each moment of your daily life. Mindfulness helps you touch the wonders of life for self-nourishment and healing." A hallmark of mindfulness is the silencing of the mind, giving way to the expanding expression of the heart in the all-knowing present moment. In that stillness there emerges a sacred connection to all.

My own unfolding journey into teaching from the heart of mindfulness originally took shape as a survivor's guide. That's right, my very own survivor's guide! While teaching at an international school in India, I had a student so challenging that I contemplated quitting a gratifying career in education that had spanned over twenty-five years. This extremely intelligent nine-year-old boy, infamous as the most difficult student in the school, was variously labeled as exhibiting Oppositional Defiant Disorder (ODD) and Attention Deficit Hyperactivity Disorder (ADHD), according to the parlance of the day. He was quick to get involved in discussions but spoke out impulsively without regard to other students' opinions; more typical was such disruptive behavior as physically harming other students or damaging school material. Fellow teachers were surprised that I kept a positive attitude, and administrators considered my teaching strategies successful: the student was received in kindness and he was progressing academically.

From an educational standpoint my teaching appeared to meet with success, but I was left exhausted and depleted at the end of each school day. Something wasn't right. The challenge was not about the student anymore, it was about me. My determination to turn my teaching day into one that also nourished me led me to search for a new working definition of teacher success: *effective student learning coupled with a deepening sense of wholeness and well-being in me, the teacher.* Thus authentic teacher success in the classroom had to include being nourished and supported in my own journey. Interestingly, mindfulness practices had been a core part of my life's journey for longer than I had even been teaching. How could I encourage qualities I was trying to cultivate in my personal life—gratitude, warmheartedness, and kindness—into my teaching life? These ethical qualities always brought more lightness and a growing sense of wholeness. Yet at the end of a school day, I was feeling quite the opposite. There was an apparent disconnect between my personal life and my teaching life. I had to make a profound shift, but how?

This dilemma resonated as a call for action and self-transformation. As a mindfulness practitioner with a long-standing meditation routine, I thought I should be able to intentionally integrate these ethical qualities and others into the way I approached my teaching day. A quality that I was cultivating in my mindfulness practices at home was working on my own ability to be more compassionate. Why not integrate compassion through skillful means into my interactions with this student? Why not make the cultivation of compassion an intentional part of my teaching strategy?

My starting point was to use a technique from my teaching repertoire: the skill of reflection. When dealing with this student, I tried my best to reflect on and observe my own attitude, speech, and behavior. Was I teaching from a gentle place or one of frustration? Was I jumping to react or taking a moment to breathe and be still? Was I feeling my heart expand or close? Was my voice naturally calm or was there a tone of measured patience? Were my interactions calm or did they come with a degree of impatience? Upon analysis, it became painfully clear to me that although it appeared I was kind to the student, this demeanor required a great deal of effort on my part. My kindness was clearly born out of frustration and measured patience. My breath rarely stilled; rather, it was strained and unsteady, mirroring my attitude toward this demanding student.

Reflecting on my own attitude and behavior from this place of non-judgment reinforced my ability to mindfully connect the act of teaching while cultivating compassion in my interactions with this student. This very connection propelled a dramatic shift. My kindness now came more directly from my heart, less forced and more embracing. My breath began to flow effortlessly, mirroring a newfound acceptance of this student, the circumstances, and my ability to receive them with grace. I felt more nourished, and an inner reservoir of strength and energy emerged from an authentic place within. Frustration melted into deep gratitude for this student coming into my life, opening my heart and my capacity to feel even more compassion. The dynamics had shifted, and a growing sense of well-being and wholeness were palpable, not just in me but, surprisingly, in the student as well. He became more accepting and responsive, staying more focused and engaged in classroom activities. In short, increased and more effective student learning occurred. This experience, in turn, deepened my mindfulness practice, especially in nurturing more compassion in me and expanding a heartfelt sense of well-being, both in and out of the classroom.

The disconnect between my personal life and my teaching life was lessening. How could I help this shift bring me to a firmer, more mindfully grounded approach to teaching? As I continued to bring more awareness to these questions, a new student, a young teenage girl from a culture in which girls and boys are schooled separately, entered the American Embassy School in New Delhi, where I was teaching. She was accustomed to a more traditional environment in which learning by rote, reciting long passages, and not looking the teacher in the eye were the norm. The American style of education, which encourages student–centered learning, thinking for oneself, and collaborating with classmates, was still unknown to her. How could I be grounded in a mindfulness-based teaching approach with this student?

As I contemplated this question, the quality of acceptance came to mind. My goal for this new student was for her to feel totally accepted and embraced for who she was as she navigated the still-unfamiliar cultural expectations in her new school. Helping this young teenager make the transition by taking on more responsibility for her own learning, as expected in most American schools, meant gently and discreetly reminding her of certain expectations. Out of class, as part of the school day, I prompted her to go to her locker, get out her books, and gather any needed materials. In class, with even more discretion, I helped her stay on track by walking by her desk and pointing to the paragraph in the book we were discussing or handing her needed material to be prepared for group work. This simple prompting, done with respect and care, helped her take the first steps to think independently and begin to take responsibility for her own learning—two brand-new concepts to her. Shortly thereafter, as she became more familiar with routines and expectations, my prompting decreased until it wasn't needed at all. In time, she began to feel confident and comfortable enough to voice her opinions in class activities and to work in cooperative groups with boys. When I accepted this student at her own level, she felt supported and affirmed for who she was. This in turn promoted this student's positive attitude, benefiting her learning and navigating a new school culture.

Now that the lens of acceptance had become a useful tool for approaching mindfulness-based teaching at school, I intentionally integrated acceptance into my mindfulness practices after the school day ended. Cultivating acceptance honed my own ability to accept and embrace whatever came up in my home practice and, indeed, in my life with family and friends. Reinforcing my own capacity to be more accepting not only improved this same quality in me but also made me a better teacher.

In reviewing the way I integrated compassion and acceptance in these two classroom examples, I began to understand compassion and acceptance as calming qualities that open the heart and deepen a mindfulness practice. I discovered that these two qualities could be deliberately integrated into my teaching strategy. I then began to view kindness, gratitude, perseverance, and other ethical qualities—qualities that nourish a growing sense of wholeness, are universal in nature, and make us better human beings—as mindfulness qualities with which to address daily classroom challenges. The qualities seemed boundless and helped me to merge my personal and professional lives as one. Further, integrating mindfulness as a way of being and teaching diminished the dichotomies between the teacher self and the personal self—the daughter, spouse, sibling, friend, or any other self. Thus began the journey of teaching from the heart of mindfulness and developing a mindfulness-based teaching approach.

My next step was to link the experiential process of practicing mindfulness to a step-by-step professional protocol in the classroom. Mindfulness and its many qualities needed to be infused into every stage of teaching—lesson planning, classroom delivery, and assessment. I needed to develop this as a cognitive process, instilling in myself a deliberate awareness and conscious decision-making procedure. I implemented different iterations of draft designs in my own classrooms, and colleagues tested out these designs.

Over the course of several years, a mindfulness-based teaching approach took shape. It is articulated as the HEARTS Mindfulness-Based Teaching Approach and is addressed from different angles in two sections of this book. In the first section, A Mindful Journey, real case studies in a variety of classroom situations are presented through the lens of the HEARTS Mindfulness-Based Teaching Approach, while an overview and instructions for its use are found in the second section, the appendix.

Mindfulness as a positive, forward-moving action, stemming from a discerning heart, expansive and healing in nature, is the starting point from which the rest of the book flows. You are invited to use the book as a professional tool, reference guide, a set of personal and classroom practices in mindfulness, as an inspiration, or in whatever ways best resonate. A Mindful Journey presents ten chapters through a variety of themes that mirror the path of an archetypal hero's journey, revealing different qualities of mindfulness as the journey unfolds. Each theme cultivates a spaciousness of mind and an expansiveness of the heart rather than a linear experience primarily of the intellect—the logical thinking mind that is so engaged in a typical teaching day. Each chapter begins with a mindfulness practice related to that chapter's theme. I have followed these practices myself for many years and have also guided others in their use, particularly while I was living on the Indian subcontinent. They are included to invite you, first and foremost, into the expansive nature of mindfulness practice and to encourage this space to grow stronger and deeper. This spaciousness of heart and mind better supports a mindfulness-based teaching approach and is more easily brought into the classroom in a seamless linking of personal practice with professional teaching. Even though the mindfulness practices are meant primarily as self-practice, teachers can easily adapt them for classroom use with students, thereby using the mindfulness practices found in these chapters as specific activities that build mindfulness as well as social and emotional skills in the classroom.

The chapters proceed by presenting real classroom situations based on my own teaching experiences, though names are fictitious. These examples span the globe as well as teaching contexts: from teaching primary grades in international schools to teaching graduate-level courses in the United States. They are all presented through the lens of HEARTS and illustrate the power of a mindfulness-based teaching approach through narratives and real classroom challenges. Each chapter's mindfulness quality is highlighted as a starting point and then followed by specific steps to identify classroom challenges and to intentionally integrate the mindfulness quality and classroom teaching strategies for effectively meeting the classroom challenge. Student learning is assessed after the classroom challenge has been met, and lastly, pausing to self-reflect ensures deeper insights of each person's own journey into mindfulness.

The appendix includes several mindfulness-based interventions. Three of them are reproducible teacher resources and support a mindfulness-based teaching approach. They are adaptable to a variety of settings: individual teachers integrating mindfulness in their classes; school-wide initiatives or curriculum development based on mindfulness in education or social and emotional learning; and larger programs for training mindful teachers. Mindful Prayer Flags and the Mindful BREATH Acrostic can be hung in classrooms as visual reminders, while Mindful Fun is likened to a game of I Spy. For those educators interested in implementing the HEARTS Mindfulness-Based Teaching Approach in their own settings, its six-step process is explained in detail along with the accompanying reproducible teacher resource tool.

The application of HEARTS to real-life classroom situations is found in each chapter. These classroom vignettes can be read in any order, and although the mindfulness practices that precede them can also be read in any order, each practice builds on and complements the previous ones and is presented sequentially. More importantly, this reading experience hopes to support professional teacher development while inviting in a spaciousness of mind and an expansiveness of heart, shifting mindfulness away from something you do and encouraging mindfulness as a way of *being*, a way of becoming.

At the heart of mindfulness rests the ever-present wholeness of being—accessible once the thinking mind has calmed down, when logic and intellect have found a respite. The heart of mindfulness cannot be unlocked with a busy monkey mind; instead it opens up when a spaciousness of mind has been cultivated, while the heart within the heart, that unstuck nature of the heart, rests in silent waiting. In Eastern philosophy, the top of the head is often symbolized by the moon. Just as the luminescent light of the moon is not generated by the moon itself but by the reflection of the sun's light, so too a still mind, where thoughts have abated to hold the fullness of the present in a spacious emptiness, reflects the light of a loving heart. The heart of mindfulness—a sacred, ever-expanding expression of the heart—is felt by an increased sense of wholeness, unity, love, and well-being. Its telltale signs are a growing manifestation of a healing nature marked by compassion, loving-kindness, gratitude, warmheartedness, and joyful happiness.

The daily act of teaching, when approached with an invitation to grow in spaciousness of mind and expansiveness of heart, allows us to delve deeper into what is present and to ask what lessons this journey brings. With ever-increasing demands from 24/7 connectivity, it is vitally important to seek a sense of balance between our internal and external worlds.

The kind of energy we put into a task is also the energy we are nourishing in ourselves, as well as what ultimately gets communicated to our students. With each step we take in teaching from the heart of mindfulness, we become more grounded in our true nature—essentially love—and then we are better able to communicate that love to all those we encounter, especially our students. In touching our students' lives from this warmhearted core of who we are, we become true peacemakers. Ultimately each person's journey is unique. By sharing our journeys we nourish our own. I hope my journey of cultivating teaching from the heart of mindfulness, shared in these pages, lends inspiration to yours.

TEACHING

from the

HEART

of

MINDFULNESS

A MINDFUL JOURNEY

I start my journey with empty hands and expectant heart.

—RABINDRANATH TAGORE

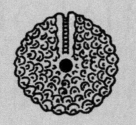

1
COURAGE

As your will is, so is your deed. As your deed is,
so is your destiny.

—BRIHADARANYAKA UPANISHAD

Mindfulness Practice

COME INTO A COMFORTABLE SEATED
POSITION. The mindfulness practice of sitting
begins with the very act of sitting. Take a moment
to acknowledge the courage just to come to the
practice. Invite in an awareness of the body as it set-
tles into the sitting posture you've chosen: this can
be seated in a chair, cross-legged on a cushion, or
another position of your choice. Examine exactly
how you take the seat. Are your sit bones, the bones

under the flesh of your buttocks, making contact with your seat? Are the sit bones weighted equally from the base? Move the weight of the body forward, then a bit backward, then left and right. Do you press into one place more than another? Make any needed adjustments to feel your base is in better alignment. This base of support is what holds the posture steady throughout the sitting practice. Inquire, take a moment, be curious, and bring awareness as you become more observant of your base. Your mind-body connection increases with this keen inquiry. With even more acute attention, find the exact spot where your body feels totally straight. Subtle movements can be felt and fine-tuned to increase your sense of balance and strength in sitting.

Now check that your body is actively engaged. This is done by gently squeezing the muscles in and up from the middle of your base and below the abdomen. The body, rather than being floppy, is actively engaged. Oftentimes more firmness and strength holds the frame of the body more easily. The engaged muscles from the base keep the body, and therefore the mind, actively alert. In sitting practice, an alert but relaxed connection of mind and body is maintained. This is sitting with ease. Coming into sitting is always fresh, always new; and when you do so with concentrated attention, it has already become a mindfulness practice.

NOW DRAW ATTENTION TO YOUR SPINE. Invite in keen observation and questioning: Is the spine straight? Can you elongate it more? Does the elongation naturally broaden the chest and expand the rib cage on all sides? Does the elongation automatically soften and widen the shoulders? With the spine lengthened, take a moment to become more aware of any growing sense of space, either physical or emotional, that has been created. Now check the neck. Is it straight or leaning forward? Sense the position of your neck and head in relationship to your shoulders. One way to do this is to check the location of your ears in relationship to the shoulders. Are the ears more in front of the shoulders? Are they behind the shoulders? Or are they directly above the shoulders? When the ears are directly above the shoulders, the upper chest, neck, and head tend to be in a more correct vertical posture and the spine is better aligned. Make any comfortable adjustments to encourage this posture. Do you feel more length in the upper body? Is there more space in the lower body? What changes can you feel in the overall sitting posture?

NOW ALLOW THE CHIN TO BE PARALLEL TO THE FLOOR. Then tuck the chin slightly under so that the cervical spine is in better alignment. Notice any shifts or differences before moving to the hands. There are several options for the placement of the hands; choose any gesture that is familiar and comfortable. With the left hand palm up in your lap, you may want to rest the right hand, palm up, in the palm of the left hand, or you may want to place the backs of both hands on each upper thigh. Whatever placement of the hands you choose, check that it encourages a strong back and soft heart in a relaxed yet ever alert posture.

JUST AS YOU CONNECT TO THE POSTURE OF THE OUTER BODY, invite in a similar connection to the inner body by bringing your awareness to the breath. As you take the next few breaths, sit in silent observation. Sense the breath. Become familiar with the breath. The breath now becomes the focus of attention. There is no need to change anything: the breath, just as it is. Continue to observe the breath for a few more minutes. Sitting in a mindfulness practice invites both time and space to become available. It may mean carving out time from outward day-to-day activities in order to ensure an inner practice. In today's fast-paced, multitasking environment, it may take more courage than ever before to find this time for self. So as you breathe in and out, take in this courage: the courage to stop, create space, give time, and use energy to sit. Feel the boldness of this courage growing inside with each breath. On each inhalation feel the lungs expand outward. On the exhalation, release any stress that the mind or body may be holding. This letting go encourages relaxation with every exhalation. Breathe in—expanding with a sense of strength and feeling more energized; breathe out—becoming lighter and more relaxed. Encourage a greater sense of taking in the breath, connect to the courageous conviction to sit and practice mindfulness. By taking this seat, each inhalation and each exhalation invites more balance and wholeness. You touch a deeper part of yourself. Each inhalation. Each exhalation. Inhale and exhale, inhale and exhale, and continue for a few more minutes: breathe in with courage and exhale into growing strength.

NOW DIRECT THE BREATH TO THE SOLAR PLEXUS, the place just above the belly and below the sternum. Inhale as the belly rises and exhale as the diaphragm sinks in. However, if you observe that the belly sinks in on the inhalation and expands on the exhalation, attempt to redirect your breathing. If it is comfortable, you can do this by expanding the belly on the inhalation as you bring air into the lungs and diaphragm; then, on the exhalation as air is released, let the belly contract and sink in. Inhale, belly expanding. Exhale, belly contracting. Inhale and exhale. This core of your being, at the solar plexus, takes in courage and exhales into a deep sense of strength. Inhale courage, exhale into more strength. Inhale and exhale, inhale and exhale. Continue for a few more breaths, breathing in with courage and exhaling as you grow in strength. Your breath invites you to stay with this practice as long as the mind stays focused. Though thoughts arise as they naturally will, every time you bring a wandering thought back to the breath, the focus of attention, recognize the courage it takes to do so. How much fun to wander with each thought! It takes courage to muster the strength to come back to the focus of attention, in this case the breath. Each time you do so, honor the courage inside yourself, thus building even more courage and conviction. Breathe in courage, exhale into strength—embody both courage and strength with every breath.

AS YOU CONTINUE TO OBSERVE THE BREATH, BRING A SOFT AWARENESS BACK to the sitting posture. Check that the muscles are engaged but at the same time relaxed. Alert and relaxed body, alert and relaxed mind. Make any necessary adjustments. Review, check, and recheck: sitting—proper alignment, engaged muscles, a strong back affirming a strong commitment to the practice, strength in the spine giving way to a softening and opening of heart and mind. And now, again, back to the breath. Observe the breath, breathe in and out. Notice. Be with that. Feelings. Thoughts. Sensations. Observe. Bring awareness to the practice without changing anything. Sit with whatever arises. Breathe in, breathe out, and continue on for several more moments. This seemingly simple act of sitting becomes a powerful mindfulness practice, one that takes commitment and courage. It requires much effort. Focus of attention: posture, alignment; muscle engagement and breath. Always vigilant, with as much concentrated attention as possible. Continue with a few more rounds of focusing on the breath.

WHEN YOU ARE READY, BEGIN TO TRANSITION OUT OF THE PRACTICE BY TAKING A DEEPER BREATH. As you bring greater awareness to the breath, embody a deep sense of courage and strength gained in the mindfulness practice. Connect to the courage, strength, and conviction you have generated. This courageous step builds a sense of purpose for sitting practice and all mindfulness practices. Now, begin to externalize the senses and become more aware of the outer environment and the sounds around you. Take a moment to acknowledge and honor the time and energy you have dedicated to this mindfulness practice: Sitting. Affirm the space you have just held sacred and the effort you have made to integrate mindfulness into your very being, naturally cultivating teaching from the heart of mindfulness. And when you are ready, gently open your eyes, greeting the world from a deeper place of courage, of greater spaciousness of mind and expansiveness of heart.

Teaching holds a mirror to the soul.

—Parker J. Palmer

Mindful Teaching

Being a heroine or hero on the journey takes courage: courage to look inward, courage to face challenges, courage to surrender to the unknown. Being aware of possessing courage brings strength to the traveler and faith in the journey.

Lucia was a cheerful, outgoing ten-year-old English-language learner from Peru. When Lucia came into the classroom, she went straight to the reading corner, plumped herself down on the carpet, and began to read to herself or any other student who happened to be walking by. During teacher read-aloud time, Lucia was always the first to raise her hand, intently following the story and offering additional details and information. But when it came to writing, although she produced pages of written stories filled with wonderful adventures, it was hard to understand her ideas or to discern a clear story line. Even Lucia could not make sense of what she had written. She would spell the same word three different ways in the same sentence, and the sentences were so ungrammatical that the meaning was obscure. When Lucia became aware that her teachers couldn't understand what she had written, she seemed at a loss, and her confidence began to plummet. The classroom challenge was for Lucia to bring greater awareness to her writing process, especially to spelling and grammar.

As a native Spanish speaker, Lucia was confused by many of the English vowels—specifically, their names, sounds, and corresponding spelling. For example, in English the name of the letter *i* is pronounced as the English long-i, but in Spanish the name of the letter *i* is pronounced like the English long-e. To add to her confusion, while almost all sounds in Spanish have one sound-to-letter correspondence in their spelling (e.g., the short-i sound is spelled [i]); in English the sound of a long-e can be spelled six different ways: [ea], [ee], [ei], [ie], and [ey]). In terms of word order, English has a standard subject + verb + object sentence structure, while in Spanish the subject, verb, and object can switch in any order. All this probably added to Lucia's confusion, and I felt that my job was to help her make sense of the English language—to build order out of chaos. I planned to start with concentrating on the building blocks of a strong foundation: decoding sounds with their corresponding spelling and writing simple, grammatically correct sentences. I hoped to achieve this while keeping Lucia's enthusiasm and sense of well-being intact. I wanted Lucia to muster the courage she would need in order to face the challenge, so courage became the mindfulness quality that I intentionally integrated into my strategy.

Lucia made exceptionally speedy progress in listening and speaking in English. She was comfortable speaking in English, she happily communicated her ideas when speaking, and she was easily understood by others. However, her phonemic awareness and her writing skills were just emerging, and I believed more focused modeling would be beneficial. The main classroom teaching strategy I chose was to work with manageable chunks of information. Focusing on a few doable skills that were quickly achievable would help Lucia find immediate success rather than feel overwhelmed by her many mistakes. Equally important, focusing on manageable chunks of information would help maintain Lucia's enthusiasm and motivation—key factors in second-language acquisition.

The classroom teaching strategy took effect in writer's workshop when Lucia and I had our daily teacher's conference. Specifically, we would record three things on Lucia's Writing Conference List that she did well; for example, (1) Correct use of capital letters in the title; (2) Good opening line; and (3) Correct use of the past-tense went. I would also write down two very specific items to work on, such as: (1) Remember that [ea] was one way of writing the long-e sound; and (2) Use a capital letter at the beginning of each sentence. New items would only be added to Lucia's list after she mastered these.

The positive results in Lucia's learning were evident in a variety of ways and throughout the process. The classroom teaching strategies helped Lucia achieve an accomplishable task, gaining success and confidence to tackle the next areas of focus without feeling the despair and confusion she had initially experienced. She eagerly delighted in reviewing her Writing Conference List and seeing the two items she was working on move to the category of skills she did well. This process served as a tangible means for Lucia to actually feel her accomplishments. Slowly but surely, there was progress in Lucia's writing. Although it took her time to write a coherent sentence, Lucia's enthusiasm remained. Eventually she progressed to the point where students, teachers, and her parents could easily understand her written stories. With steady effort, courage, and unwavering persistence, Lucia made it through the chaos and complexity of language acquisition and reached a higher level of proficiency.

Even at her young age, Lucia managed to tap into her courage, bringing forbearance and patience to a formidable task. My self-reflection on this classroom challenge fuels my faith to reach for and touch the wellspring of courage that is always deep inside, especially during times of confusion and self-doubt. Building courage represents small but significant steps to more solid ground—moving ever forward, progressing toward a sense of order, strength, and wholeness.

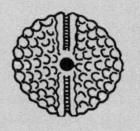

KINDNESS

Everyone is kneaded out of the same dough,
but not baked in the same oven.

—YIDDISH PROVERB

Mindfulness Practice

COME INTO A COMFORTABLE POSITION, either sitting on a chair or lying down on the floor. Whichever position you have chosen, gently rest your hands on your belly and then close your eyes. This strengthens a growing mind-body connection with breath awareness. Closed eyes encourage an inward attention from outward distractions. Now invite in a full cycle of breathing: a complete in-breath and a complete out-breath. With ever-increasing awareness of the breath, feel a growing sense of kindness, and invite in a spaciousness of mind and an expansiveness of heart as you transition into today's mindfulness practice: Belly Breath.

GENTLY NOTICE THAT AS YOU DRAW THE BREATH IN through both nostrils, the belly rises. On the exhalation, the belly falls inward while the air is released through your nose. Feel your belly moving with the breath. Breathe in through the nose, belly rising; breathe out through your nose, belly falling. It is a gentle, natural breath as you inhale and exhale. A calm breath: in, belly rising; out, belly falling. If you notice your stomach going in on the inhalation and out on the exhalation and if it feels comfortable, reverse the breath so that air coming into the lungs on the inhalation fills and expands the belly, and as air gets exhaled, the belly and diaphragm contract. As your focus of attention is drawn to the incoming breath, feel the belly rise, and on the outgoing breath, feel the belly fall. You may want to visualize your belly as a balloon filling up with air and expanding from all sides on the inhalation and then deflating as air goes out on the exhalation. Inhale a sense of freshness, vitality, and energy with the increased amount of oxygen, and with the exhalation gently let go of tension, naturally ridding the body of toxins.

WITH EACH INHALATION, VITALITY REACHES THE WARMTH OF THE BELLY. As the belly expands with this sense of vitality, connect to a deeper space within. Slowly release the breath on the exhalation, and with it release tension and stress. Again, focus on bringing the breath in, at its own pace and rhythm, as the belly rises. And as the breath gathers deep in the belly, you may perceive a growing space, a pause, a gap between the inhalation and exhalation. Then, when the outgoing breath begins, it starts from this deep place of calm, from this gap between the inhalation and exhalation, gathering up any tension and stress ready to be released. A natural lengthening of the breath may match a growing calmness. Watch the breath, feel the belly. Inhale as the belly rises, exhale as the belly releases, and stay with each breath with growing awareness.

THE BELLY BREATH, WITH EACH INHALATION and exhalation, helps bring you back to yourself, with gentleness, with kindness. This smooth and gentle breath, the belly rising and falling, draws in this kindness, a loving-kindness toward self. Welcome each incoming breath, filled with light and love, to rest deep in the belly. Then, with a naturalness of ease, the breath removes unneeded tension and stress on each exhalation. The breath, a kindness, a tenderness of self, available always, breathing in and breathing out, belly rising and falling. Awareness of the breath with a gentle tenderness of loving-kindness. Breathe in and breathe out. Breathe in and breathe out.

WITH THIS GROWING AWARENESS, INVITE IN A SENSE OF CALM AND KINDNESS. There is a comfort in knowing that this ability to bring the breath to the belly as it rises and then to release on every exhalation is a tool that is always accessible. Breathing in, belly rising; breathing out, belly falling: a technique to put into practice when you want to nourish an inner sense of calm and kindness. The belly breath encourages relaxation and cultivates a growing sense of mindfulness.

WHEN YOU ARE READY, LET GO OF THE FOCUS ON THE BREATH and transition out of the practice by resting in a place of growing relaxation, an ease of just being, without doing anything. Enjoy this moment, a pause from the inner to the outer, integrating the two as one. Belly breath—a source of increased well-being, always available, always accessible. And when you are ready, begin to externalize the senses, become more aware of the outer environment and the sounds around you. Take a moment to acknowledge and honor the time and energy you have dedicated to this mindfulness practice: Belly Breath. Affirm the space you have just held sacred and the effort you have made to integrate mindfulness into your very being, naturally cultivating teaching from the heart of mindfulness. And when you are ready, gently open your eyes, greeting the world from a deeper place of kindness, a greater spaciousness of mind and expansiveness of heart.

Education should be in harmony with the child's essentially kind nature. The most important element is that children be raised in a climate of love and tenderness. Although from an ideal perspective human qualities ought to be developed in conjunction with kindness, I often say that if I had to choose between important general qualities and kindness, I believe I would choose kindness.

—His Holiness The XIV Dalai Lama

Mindful Teaching

When we can touch that genuine place where loving-kindness resides deep within and freely shower it on others, its essence of love and kindness grows even stronger in us.

Tens of thousands of students, in the U.S. alone, wake up each morning too afraid to go to school for fear of being bullied. Bullying, for both the victim and the bully, is a complicated issue that should always be addressed, never ignored. In one of my language arts classes, I witnessed ongoing interaction between two middle-school-aged boys that made it alarmingly clear to me: I had both a bully, Royce, and the person being bullied, Derek, in my class. Royce's underlying aggression toward Derek, and Derek's feelings of hopelessness, fear, and lack of confidence clearly exemplified a pattern of bullying and being bullied. Though I could intervene when I noticed something obvious, bullies often wait until an adult isn't watching to be the most aggressive. I knew I had to do something beyond those moments when I could intervene, so my immediate classroom challenge was to address this situation of bullying and take action.

There is a wealth of information about how to stop bullying. Some proactive steps for highly sensitive boys and girls include building up their confidence, physical strength, ability in self-defense, and other strategies from a very young age. One direct intervention is for adults to harshly discipline the bully, while some studies suggest that bullying is a transitory stage and so counseling should be the priority. There are other strategies; for example, the victim might use an "I message" or confidently communicate an ability that the bully can't match. U.S. states have specific laws against bullying, including laws against bullying via social media, and private schools like mine have a strong anti-bullying policy.

Even with all this background information and the school policy being followed, I felt that an additional, more heart-to-heart approach would be beneficial.

More specifically, I felt a need to touch a place of kindness, connecting both the bully and the victim with a sense of shared experience and shared humanity. By helping to make this connection through kindness, I intentionally integrated kindness as the mindfulness quality to cultivate. Over the next several weeks, I worked with the entire class to build background knowledge and vocabulary related to various areas such as mindfulness, loving-kindness, visualizations, and conflict resolution in order for them to have a lived experience of loving-kindness. The first mindfulness-based exercises we practiced were centered on breath awareness. For example, we practiced belly breath with students, identifying feelings and emotions around moods, behavior, and reactions to situations. To focus more directly on conflict resolution, I used several books and stories in the language arts class that highlighted how the main characters, though they began with mutual distrust, apprehension, and even disdain, reached resolution by being empathetic and by connecting to and respecting others in a compassionate manner. These books and stories helped set a context for the classroom community as well as vocabulary and points of reference for discussion. Finally, I did a guided visualization for students to experience silently. To prepare them for this, I presented different mind-maps and visual tools so students could confidently begin brainstorming their ideas in writing immediately after the visualization. These preliminary techniques were in preparation for my main classroom teaching strategy: a visualization on loving-kindness.

Now I was ready to lead my students through the visualization. I let them know that after the visualization they would brainstorm ideas that came up during the visualization and these ideas would be used for their next piece of writing. They were also instructed to remain quiet after the visualization and to brainstorm their ideas by using their mind-maps and write these ideas down in silence. After answering a few questions, I guided my students through the following visualization:

1. Think of a place where you feel safe. It can be one of your favorite places, like the beach, a tree house, your room, or a vacation spot you have visited. See yourself there: calm, quiet, and peaceful. Now envelop yourself with love, understanding, and kindness. Try to actually feel how you feel and totally accept yourself as you are. Remain like that for a few moments.

2. Now think of the people you love the most. Visualize them. You may see members of your family, a friend, or a group of friends. You can even visualize a pet. Whomever or whatever you choose, connect to your deep sense of love and kindness. Try to feel how they are feeling, empathize with them, and then surround them with love, understanding, and kindness. Remain in that bubble of kindness for a few moments. Really feel how your kindness is being showered on them.

3. Now think of someone you might see every day but may not really know. This could be the bus driver, a student from another class, the janitor, or someone at a store or restaurant. Though you may be strangers, give them your kindness and understanding. Wish them the best and hope that they feel happy and loved. Be with this feeling for a few moments.

4. Now think of someone you may be having difficulty with, someone you may not like, or even someone who is causing you harm. See if you can direct that same sense of love and kindness you have shown others to this person. Try to empathize with this person,

knowing in your heart of hearts that everyone wants to feel safe, everyone wants to feel
loved, and everyone wants kindness given to
them. It is as if you are inviting this person to
step into a space of love and safety. Stay with
this feeling as long as you can.

5. Finally, bring your attention to the natural
    world around you: the gardens, the birds, the
    sky. Surround the natural world, the entire
    world, everywhere on Earth, in a ball of love,
    kindness, and brotherhood. What do you see?
    How do you feel? Connect to what you see
    and feel for a few more moments. Then, when
    you are ready, take a few breaths and open
    your eyes. Begin brainstorming and write
    your experience and any ideas while remain-
    ing in silence.

During the visualization, a soft peace settled into
the classroom, and the students' feelings became
powerfully palpable. When the students opened
their eyes and began to write, this lived experience
of feeling loving-kindness, to whatever degree each
of the students may have felt it, seemed manifest.
After fifteen minutes of writing in silence and letting
that calm grow deeper, the class reconvened for a

final few minutes to share their brainstorming ideas before the end of class.

When the class met the next day, there was a dramatic shift in the interaction between Royce and Derek, and in the class as a whole. Over the next several days all the students, including Royce, seemed more sensitive and more respectful; all of the students seemed to better self-regulate their own behavior as well as monitor Royce. This positive change of attitude and behavior continued throughout the school year, and the class more actively interacted with Derek, and did so in a caring, kindly manner. The whole social environment improved as Royce no longer had to show off his powerful status and Derek no longer had to feel powerless and afraid. I believe that both Royce and Derek touched on their own genuine kindness, experiencing a truer part of themselves. The classroom atmosphere was greatly enhanced and the focus on learning much more evident. The results in student learning touched both Royce and Derek in positive ways, just as they did for the entire classroom community.

The story of Royce and Derek reminds me to be ever vigilant of those who are victims as well as those who, though outwardly negative in their behavior, seek kindness and understanding as well. Both are suffering in their own way, and both benefit from kindness. I can bring this self-reflection to my own situation by asking: When I'm interacting with seemingly difficult people, do I remain kind? Am I kinder and gentler with myself at key times in my life? Surely, when I connect in loving-kindness, I automatically soften, I feel connected to those I love, to those I may not know, and to those whom I know are struggling. My heart opens and I feel more connected to the entire world around me, for the thread of loving-kindness connects us all in joy and sorrow, healing us through compassion and love.

3

ACCEPTANCE

Feelings come and go like clouds in a windy sky.
Conscious breathing is my anchor.

—THICH NHAT HANH

Mindfulness Practice

COME INTO A COMFORTABLE SEATED POSI-
TION, place your hands on your thighs or in your lap,
and gently close your eyes. Check that you are seated
firmly by activating a strong spine, naturally opening the chest and softening your heart. Smile gently
from the outer creases of your eyes and mouth. Take
a moment and bring awareness to one full cycle of
breathing: a complete in-breath and a complete out-
breath. With ever-increasing awareness of the breath,

feel a growing sense of acceptance of self and invite in a spaciousness of mind and an expansiveness of heart as you transition into today's mindfulness practice: Anchor Breath.

WITH INCREASED FOCUS OF ATTENTION ON THE IN-BREATH AND THE OUT-BREATH, invite in the opportunity for your mind to feel more calm and your physical body more relaxed. Observe any sensations as you continue to bring awareness to the in-breath and out-breath: inhale and exhale, inhale and exhale. As you continue the practice of breathing in and breathing out, draw your attention to the stomach area. Breathe in, stomach rising; breathe out, stomach falling. Without changing anything, bring your awareness to how your stomach rises and then falls as you breathe in and out. Bring a sharpened awareness to observe the stomach rising and falling, rising and falling. With an even greater focus of attention, connect to the sensations and feelings of the stomach rising and falling, rising and falling. The entire stomach area, rising and falling. Feel this entire region as your base; draw the breath into this base, connect to the strength of the in-breath and the release of the out-breath; draw in strength and energy, release stress and agitation. Breathe in, stomach rising; breathe out, stomach falling. Draw in relaxation and calm, release fatigue and stress. Breathe in and breathe out, breathe in and breathe out.

FEEL ANCHORED IN THE IN-BREATH AND OUT-BREATH, RISING AND FALLING. Observe the growing sense of calm and relaxation. Breathe in and breathe out. As you feel more and more anchored in this breath, invite the breath to become your anchor. Breathe in and breathe out, breathe in and breathe out. Think of the breath as your inner anchor, connected to the breath. With every in-breath and with every out-breath your anchor is with you at all times. Just like an anchor, it always holds you steady. Breathe in and breathe out. Breathe in and breathe out.

IMAGINE AN ANCHOR WHICH KEEPS A SHIP STEADY—no matter the prevailing conditions. Each breath is an added link to the anchor's chain, keeping the ship afloat while the anchor remains secure in the deep ocean bed. With each lengthening of the breath, the deeper the anchor reaches. The ship, floating on the water's surface, impervious to the outer conditions. The links to the anchor increase to reach the deeper depths of self. The breath, keeping you steady, keeping you anchored in your base. Breathe in and breathe out, breathe in and breathe out. The anchor keeps the ship moored through wind and rain just like your anchor breath can keep you steady and calm through any disturbances of the day and the storms of life.

THINK OF YOURSELF AS THAT SHIP, SAILING THROUGH LIFE'S CHALLENGES but always with your anchor breath, breathe in and breathe out, breathe in and breathe out. Being anchored to calm, being anchored to an inner serenity and sense of stillness. Anchor breath. The image of a ship—sometimes with gentle waves, at other times, choppy ones; smooth sailing on sunny days, being tossed and turned on stormy days, but the anchor always there to keep the ship steadier. Your anchor breath, keeping you safely moored to your source of greater equanimity and balance. Breathe in and breathe out, breathe in and breathe out. Breathe in, belly rising; breathe out, belly falling. Anchor breath.

THIS STRENGTH OF BREATH, YOUR ANCHOR, WITH YOU AT ALL TIMES. Accessible always. Affirm this connection. Observe the sensations. Feel their effects. Embody this experience. Connecting to your anchor breath affirms this deep connection to self. Breathe in and breathe out. Breathe in and breathe out. Your breath, no one else's—it belongs to you and it is always there for you. Your very own anchor breath. Breathe in and breathe out, breathe in and breathe out, staying safely moored to that part of yourself through your breath. By staying anchored, a greater steadiness of self, a calmer voice, a more understanding heart, a greater acceptance of self, a more peaceful part of you surfaces. The anchor breath: breathe in and breathe out, encouraging more calm, more relaxation, keeping you attached to a deeper sense of well-being, a wholeness anchored in peace and love, an affirmation of your true nature.

AS YOU BREATH IN AND OUT, THE ANCHOR OF THE BREATH is there to connect you to a deeper sense of well-being, unstuck from the mental faculties of a stormy mind. Unstuck from the mind judging: good, bad; craving, avoiding; right, wrong. The anchor of the breath stemming from the heart's essential nature: a love that is unconditioned by judgment. This wholeness of heart welcomes and accepts all that passes before it. So breathing in, all is welcome; breathing out, all is appreciated. Acceptance. Resting in this place of heartfelt acceptance, breathing in, breathing out, breathing in, breathing out, giving way to an open acceptance of what is being observed. Witnessing. Breathing. Present-moment awareness.

WHEN YOU ARE READY, LET GO OF THE FOCUS ON THE BREATH. Begin to transition out of the practice and become more aware of the outer environment and the sounds around you. Embody a truer wholeness of self, a deeper nature of being, anchored in love, held in acceptance. Take a moment to acknowledge and honor the time and energy you have dedicated to this mindfulness practice: Anchor Breath. Enjoy this moment, a pause from the inner to the outer, integrating the two as one. Affirm the space you have just held sacred and the effort you have made to integrate mindfulness into your very being, naturally cultivating teaching from the heart of mindfulness. And when you are ready, gently open your eyes, greeting the world from a deeper place of acceptance, of greater spaciousness of mind and expansiveness of heart.

We must learn to live together as brothers or perish together as fools.

—MARTIN LUTHER KING JR.

Mindful Teaching

Acceptance stems from honoring the sacredness within. Acceptance is without judgment; for how can you be accepting if you are judging at the same time? True acceptance embraces all that is present.

Holly, an English-language learner, was an eight-year-old girl from Amsterdam. She brought sunshine and an innocent sense of life that brought magic to the world of the classroom. Her imaginative spirit seemed quite special, and her kind, gentle personality was something to admire and cherish. After the first few months of school, she had made continuous progress in all areas of second-language acquisition. As long as Holly was happy and making progress, I thought the situation was fine. However, Holly's grade-three homeroom teacher noted that Holly was academically at the lower end of the class. He seemed to feel an urgent need that Holly buckle down and get more serious about school. He communicated both his disappointment over what he determined was Holly's relatively slow progress in comparison to his others students and also his disapproval of her daydreaming and engaging in child's play during most of the school day.

The homeroom teacher communicated his observations when we met for a conference with Holly's parents. He apparently hit a nerve; Holly's parents had also noticed that Holly's older sibling had been far ahead of Holly's current academic level when he was her age. To fuel further worry, Holly's younger sibling, two grades below, was beginning to outpace Holly in her ability to read and write and in her overall interest and enthusiasm for schoolwork. Holly's parents became more worried about Holly's skills and more exasperated with Holly's lack of interest in schoolwork. The result was that Holly's parents fully supported the homeroom teacher's views.

Over the next several weeks, Holly's grade-level teacher became stricter while his tone became more disapproving and negative. Not surprisingly,

Holly became noticeably much sadder. Her growing melancholy was jeopardizing her joyful spirit. This sparked a sadness in me and with it, a determination to protect Holly's lovely spirit. I saw that my classroom challenge was to do just that: protect her spirit. And the way to do that was to demonstrate the progress Holly had already made and could continue to make. I wanted to encourage a more positive environment for her learning, which in turn would encourage still more progress. Garnering support from her home-room teacher and parents would be key to achieving my goal. I hoped it would also ensure that Holly could fully express her naturally joyful spirit.

I wanted to nourish Holly's inner world and honor the joy with which she experienced life, so the mindfulness quality that I intentionally implemented was acceptance—specifically, the acceptance of Holly's non-academic learning style. My classroom teaching strategy was to demonstrate and convincingly communicate the school progress that Holly had made thus far. My first step was to ask her homeroom teacher and parents to be more flexible in establishing the standards by which they were judging Holly and by which they were expecting her to perform. Rather than using external standards of assessment, we worked together to establish more student-centered benchmarks that encouraged Holly to progress academically while allowing her to learn in her own unique way.

The specific tool for doing this became Holly's student portfolio. This meant, for example, taking photos when Holly was engaged in imaginative play. Then I would either record Holly's voice explaining what she was doing in the photo or she would write down a description below the photo. These recordings and written descriptions were included in the portfolio on a weekly basis. In addition, the recordings and written descriptions became the main resource with which to build language skills. For example, lessons in vocabulary, spelling, and simple sentence structure could be drawn from the written descriptions. By documenting and communicating observable anecdotal and academic work in different skills areas such as speaking, listening, reading, writing, and critical thinking, in just a month's time the portfolio provided concrete evidence of Holly's continual progress in all areas to her parents and her homeroom teacher.

Over the next few months, the portfolio, created and curated by Holly, continued to be a powerful tool for showing her progress. It also allowed Holly to flourish in an environment that was more conducive to her learning style. Equally important, the homeroom teacher's attitude shifted from disapproval to active support. He now based Holly's learning on her own progress rather than comparisons to her classmates. In turn, this directly influenced Holly's parents, who soon began to celebrate her success at each step. Her parents continued to individualize their academic expectations of Holly rather than hold the same expectations they had for her siblings.

By accepting Holly—her personality, her learning style, and her readiness to learn in a typical school environment—we honored her as a person and kept her anchored in her own true nature. Rather than spiraling downward, which I felt had begun to happen, the situation was turned around; a positive, supportive learning environment ensued. Of even greater importance, Holly's joyful, innocent spirit remained intact. Her kindness and warmhearted nature were not sacrificed for the sake of faster academic progress. As evidenced by the portfolio, progress was being made in student learning, and a sense of her parents' and teacher's support brought a greater feeling of pride and encouragement.

Even years later, when I think of Holly a magic sense of joy lights my heart. How can we cherish and honor each student for who they are? Reflecting on Holly always helps me see how precious and unique each person is. To truly honor the special gifts that each student offers is a sacred privilege placed in a teacher's heart.

With self-reflection, I become more aware of certain qualities inside myself that may feel disagreeable to me! Yet being with what is present leads to a fuller acceptance of self. And a full acceptance of self is a fundamental step on the path to inner peace and happiness.

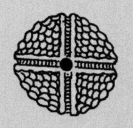

❊4❊
COMPASSION

The best we can do is lean toward the light,
toward the harmonious relationships that
come from compassion with suffering,
from understanding the other person.

—JOSEPH CAMPBELL

✸ *Mindfulness Practice*

COME INTO A COMFORTABLE SEATED POSITION
with the back of the hands resting on each thigh.
Invite in a gentle alertness of mind and body as you
allow your eyes to close. Bring awareness to one or
more full cycle of breathing: a complete in-breath and
a complete out-breath. With ever-increasing awareness of the breath, feel a growing sense of compassion,
invite in a spaciousness of mind and an expansiveness

of heart as you transition into today's mindfulness practice: Loving-Kindness.

WITH INCREASED FOCUS OF ATTENTION ON THE IN-BREATH AND THE OUT-BREATH, connect to your body sensations. Invite in the opportunity for your mind and body to relax. Settle into this increased sense of well-being. Continue to bring attention to the in-breath and out-breath: inhale, exhale, inhale, exhale The ever-expanding ease of the mind gives way to an ever-expanding opening of the heart. The heart center invites you in to connect to its core, its core of compassion, love, and kindness. Breathe in: feel the softness, the gentleness of this compassion and love. Breathe out: connect to the kindness and goodwill of the heart-nature inside of you. Breathe into every cell of your body, breathe in compassion and all-embracing, pulsating love and kindness. Breathe out as that love and kindness bathe your very being. With every in-breath and every out-breath, feel drenched in an ever-increasing, ever-tender, safe, and healing presence of love and kindness. Inhale, exhale, a loving heart. Inhale and exhale as you continue on for a few more moments.

YOUR WHOLE BEING IS INVITED TO SINK INTO THIS EVER-INCREASING, ever-expanding loving-kindness of the heart. Observe any sensations. Feel their effects. Embody this experience. This embodiment of loving-kindness can be offered outward to those you love most: family, friends, loved ones. With every in-breath, expand loving-kindness into your being; with every out-breath, shower compassion, love, and kindness onto your loved ones. With every in-breath, feel that loving-kindness expand; dedicate every out-breath to drenching your loved ones in your compassion and loving-kindness. Inhale, exhale, inhale, exhale, and continue on for several minutes. With a knowing deep inside your heart, experience your loved ones receiving your pure, heartfelt loving-kindness, reaching them and drenching them from their core in love and compassion. Inhale and exhale, inhale and exhale.

As you continue to inhale and expand in loving-kindness, continue to expand your expression of this loving-kindness; dedicate its loving, tender, kind, and healing energy to people whom you regard somewhat neutrally, with neither strong feelings of affection nor feelings of aversion or rejection. These might be people you do not know well, or people with whom you interact daily or just occasionally. Inhale and exhale, inhale and exhale, and continue on for several minutes. With every in-breath stay grounded in loving-kindness and compassion, with every out-breath feel their expansion. Compassion and loving-kindness taking such a hold that you continue to expand in its loving nature—you along with both those you love and those with whom you are less familiar, all enveloped under their umbrella of kindness and love.

AS YOU CONTINUE TO INHALE AND EXHALE, INHALE AND EXHALE, sense how the nature of loving-kindness grounds you in your own true nature—so firmly rooted in this feeling, this being in loving-kindness. It penetrates you to such an extent that the all-expansive nature of compassion and loving-kindness extends out to include those people whom you may find difficult, to those people you try to avoid or to those who evoke a negative reaction in you. Breathe in and breathe out, and again breathe in and breathe out. You are grounded in loving-kindness. You are so firmly rooted that nothing can disturb this ever-expanding love. Direct your awareness to people who bring a sense of frustration, anger, or other afflictive emotion in you; those people become the object of your compassion and loving-kindness. With each in-breath and every out-breath, continue to grow in compassion and loving-kindness. These people are now able to soak in the softness and tenderness in their own hearts from the goodwill your compassion and loving-kindness bring them. Continue to grow in your ability to embrace them. As their hearts soften and as you feel their hearts melt, yours too begins to understand, to soften, to connect. Your loving heart connects to theirs, dissolving the outer layers of armor and defenses, melting into the opening of their own true nature and your own true nature: love and kindness at its core. Breathe in and breathe out, inhale and exhale, inhale and exhale.

CONTINUE TO SEND OUT COMPASSION AND LOVING-KINDNESS AS YOU BREATHE IN AND OUT— to your loved ones, to those you hardly know, and even to those who had evoked a negative reaction in you. Now expand out to include people suffering from sickness, violence, hunger, loneliness, and other sorrows. May they also receive your loving-kindness. May this tender, compassionate energy of loving-kindness reach them and provide a deeper sense of comfort, a deeper knowing that others care, a deeper kindness and peace, a contribution to the healing of their hearts. As you breathe in and out, even the natural world—the animal kingdom, the living world of nature and beyond—may all receive and be bathed in loving-kindness. This expanded heart of loving-kindness connects all. Feel that connection. Be that connection, that unity, that oneness. May all be happy. May all be free from suffering.

When you are ready, begin to transition out of the practice by inviting in a deeper breath. As you bring greater awareness to the breath, embody a deep sense of loving-kindness: its font of peace, of love, of well-being. Embody and integrate peace and love into your being. Loving-kindness—in you, spreading outward, all-encompassing, loving-kindness. Breathe in and breathe out. Enjoy this moment, a pause from the inner to the outer, integrating the two as one. Now, with slightly more awareness of the breath as you prepare to externalize the senses, take a fuller in-breath and a fuller out-breath. Take a moment to acknowledge and honor the time and energy you have dedicated to this mindfulness practice: Loving-Kindness. Integrate this increased sense of balance and harmony—a wholeness of peace and deeper compassion. Affirm the space you have just held sacred and the effort you have made to integrate mindfulness into your very being, naturally cultivating teaching from the heart of mindfulness. When you are ready, gently open your eyes, greeting the world from a deeper place of compassion and loving-kindness, of greater spaciousness of mind and expansiveness of heart.

I suggest we look at compassion as a mode of inquiry. I believe it is possible to examine our subject matter, whatever it may be, through a glass of tenderness as well as through a glass of reason.

—MARY ROSE O'REILLY

Mindful Teaching

Compassion is the heart song that connects the universe and our place within it and throughout it. At the heart of compassion is the connection to deep suffering, the human condition. It is when we can feel this suffering and heal it with loving-kindness, in others and ourselves, that we truly cultivate compassion.

One year I taught a group of high school seniors in Ecuador who made up what was called the Remedial English Class. Several of the English teachers, including the department head, had given up teaching this group and proclaimed they were on their way to failure, risking a chance to graduate and receive a high school diploma. When the school director called me as a consultant to the school, he also begged me to take over the class. After agreeing, I soon noticed that the students showed minimal interest in the set curriculum and no motivation to read or write in English. Through class discussion, I soon learned that ten out of the thirteen students had attempted suicide. These students had attempted to disconnect from life itself, let alone care about proficiency at reading and writing! My classroom challenge was for these students to pass English class and graduate from high school. I needed to find something important enough to inspire their interest and serve as a catalyst for getting them to practice reading and writing in English.

I felt the best service I could provide this special group of individuals was a safe, compassionate place to express who they were. This meant first acknowledging their past experiences, present feelings, and hopes for the future. I needed to do this without judgment or psychological counseling. I wanted to create a classroom environment in which I could empathize and feel their suffering while allowing them to give life to their feelings and thoughts. I saw this as a basic tenet of compassion, and thus compassion became the intentional mindfulness quality.

My classroom teaching strategy was to identify a project-based theme that would be entirely conceived and implemented by the students to increase student ownership of the learning—specifically, to increase student investment in determining the curriculum and to create student-generated material. My role would be to serve as a facilitator in this process. Students began by brainstorming topics. Of the many topics, suicide was the overwhelming favorite. So we proceeded to begin researching this topic by brainstorming different aspects of suicide. Each student then chose one aspect of the topic, such as prevention or treatment, to research and present to the class. Through a process of reading, note taking, narrative, and persuasive and expository writing, as well as personal journaling throughout the project, students were ready for the final stage: a short film, "Special Report on Suicide."

During the next several weeks, there was a buzz of activity. Students were enthusiastically immersed in this project from its initial stages through its completion. They felt empowered to have a forum in which to discuss an area of their lives that held special meaning. Adding to their interest was the opportunity to learn from each other. The academic need to read and write was incidental even as, at the same time, they were practicing and improving their reading and writing skills day by day. The culminating film release in class was both emotional and celebratory. After extensive research, note taking, report writing, and then speaking on film, not only had the students' reading and writing skills dramatically improved, but a strong sense of a caring, supportive community had formed.

Immediately thereafter, the students were eager to tackle their next project-based theme. Again, they chose their topic and decided on the theme: drug trafficking. And so the year proceeded. The students continued to improve their reading and writing skills, and by the end of the year they had made great strides in their learning. Every student in class passed English and graduated from high school.

I felt privileged to become a part of this special world. I don't think I did anything differently than I would have done with any other group of students: respecting every person for who they were, and for their personal and cultural experiences, was my way of sharing myself with each individual in the class. This connected me to each one of the students, and they to me. What an honor to be a teacher and feel a deep connection to students on a daily basis! The classroom becomes an opportunity to cultivate compassion each and every day. With the lens of self-reflection, I see how tapping into this sense of compassion cultivates its growing nature in me. When truly honoring another person, the essence of compassion—"suffering-with"—is touched. In that deep connection, separation evaporates and love fills the space.

❦5❦
REFLECTION

Reflection can slowly bring us to wisdom.

—SOGYAL RINPOCHE

Mindfulness Practice

COME INTO A COMFORTABLE SEATED POSI-
TION, gently closing your eyes. Begin a full cycle
of breathing: a complete in-breath and a complete
out-breath. Breathe, in and out, in and out. With
ever-increasing awareness of the breath, continue
for a few more cycles of breathing until you feel a
growing sense of calm. Then invite in a spaciousness
of mind and an expansiveness of heart as you transition into today's mindfulness practice: Body Scan.

WITH INCREASED CONCENTRATED ATTENTION, take note of the entire physical body—its degree of stress or relaxation, from the top of the head all the way down the body to the bottom of the feet and then back again from the bottom of the feet to the top of the head. Just observe, without changing anything. Now draw an imaginary boundary around your body, a few inches away from your physical body. When this imaginary line is complete, rest in any sensations that arise. Use this observation as a starting point to today's mindfulness practice. Mentally prepare to go into the practice of scanning your body, a practice that brings acute attention and observation of your body, from top to bottom and bottom to top.

WHEN YOU ARE READY, INVITE YOUR FOCUS OF ATTENTION TO THE VERY TOP OF YOUR HEAD. Bring awareness to any sensations there. Is this area of focus as small as a pinpoint, or is it a larger area? Can you determine the weight of the area? Is there a heaviness or lightness? Is there fluidity or solidity? Is the sensation on the surface, or is it penetrating from within? Can you determine the general temperature of the area—is it hot, warm, cool, or cold? Is there a texture to the sensations? Are there any tingling or prickly sensations? Or is there any throbbing, pulsating sensation? Is there an emptiness or a hollowness? Bring full awareness, full attention, and name these sensations. Observe if there are any other sensations, or make a mental note if there is no awareness of any sensations at all. Now, gently, expand the area of awareness in a concentric circle; expand outward until it covers the entire circumference of your head. Be sure to include your face and scan the entire area of your face. As you do so, continually identify and name any sensations that arise.

NOW DRAW THE ATTENTION DOWN THE ENTIRE NECK REGION; NOTICE ITS WEIGHT AND DENSITY— heaviness or lightness, solidity or fluidity. Your attention slowly moves down and around the neck and then reaches the top of your shoulders. Identify any sensations in the shoulders and the shoulder area. Can you detect any tightness, or a sense of looseness? With even more acute attention, can you describe any other sensations? Is there any discomfort or comfort? Tension or relaxation? Any throbbing or pulsating? If so, what is its intensity? Are there some areas of noticeable sensations arising and other areas without any sensations arising? When you are ready, make your way to both upper arms, observe and name any sensations as they arise. Slowly and deliberately make your way to the elbows, lower arms, wrists, and hands.

Again, bring attention to these areas and identify any sensations. There may be a scratchiness or smoothness coming from your clothes, or perhaps a warmth or coolness of the air against the skin. Take note. Observe from a place of neutrality and equanimity, without adding any commentary or judgment. Just witness what arises. Now, resting the attention in the hands, notice both palms, and then each finger, starting with the thumbs. Can you detect any sense of heat or cold, any tingling or pulsating? What other sensations do you notice?

THE NEXT AREA OF ATTENTION IS THE BACK. Start with the upper portion of the back. Bring your attention to any areas of comfort, ease, or fluidity. Now bring your attention to any tension or discomfort. There may be areas of blockages or heaviness. Observe. Notice. Do not change anything. Experience awareness from a place of equanimity. If there is a sense of pain anywhere, is it penetrating? What is its intensity? Is there a burning sensation, a shooting pain sensation, or is the pain more generalized? Is it near the surface or deep below the surface? Does the nature of the pain change as the focus of attention remains on the sensations? Is it moving, dissolving, changing in its temperature or texture? If so, how is its nature changing? Keep noting and observing, without changing anything. Keep scanning from this place of neutral observation. Continue to scan down your back with the same focus of attention. Continue to the middle of the back and onto the lower part of the back.

As you continue to name and identify sensations, move your attention to the front of your body. Bring your attention to the top of your chest. With full awareness and acute attention, scan the top of the chest, naming sensations, their temperature, weight, texture, or any other aspect. Compare the sensations of the chest area to the area of the back. Is there a different aspect to the weight or texture of the sensations? Continue to scan the front of your body to the middle of your torso and down to the pelvic region, and eventually onto your hips. From here scan your buttocks and begin to bring the focus of attention to both upper legs. With each body part, scan slowly and deliberately; notice what arises and any sensations. Determine any sense of heaviness or lightness, tightness or openness, tension or fluidity. Is there a difference between the two legs or a difference between the lower part of the body and the upper body? Observe, take a mental note of any different sensations from a place of equanimity. Continue with this directed observation to include both knees, now lower legs, calves and shins, and then ankles and feet.

Bring your full attention to the tops of both feet and the soles of the feet, and then to each toe, starting with the big toes.

INVITE YOUR ATTENTION TO SCAN THE BODY IN REVERSE ORDER. Do so from a place of growing equanimity, reflecting without judgment on what arises. Observe. Readjust your posture if necessary, straighten your back, engage your muscles; note each and every sensation as you do so, slowly, intentionally, and with acute observation of your body and its sensations. Toes, soles of each foot, tops of the feet, ankles, lower legs, knees, upper legs, buttocks, hips. The lower part of the torso, the middle part, the heart and chest area. Note the sensations, be aware of any difference when compared to previous sensations observed. Now, scan the lower back, middle back, upper back, entire shoulder area. Again, revisit these areas with a new sense of sharpened discernment, concentrated attention, and full awareness. Notice sensations of all ten fingers, palms and tops of the hands, wrists, lower arms, elbows, upper arms, and shoulders. Now observe the neck, the entire neck region as you make your way back to the head. As you prepare to bring the body scan to completion, invite your penetrating attention to focus on sensations around the surface of your face, the back and sides of the head, and the top of the head. Slowly and deliberately make you way to the exact place at the very top of the head where you first began. When you are ready, gently release your focus of attention from your physical body. Invite your awareness back to the imaginary outline of your body. Take a moment and compare any sensations to when you first did this.

When you are ready, begin to transition out of the practice by letting go of any specific focus of attention and rest in a place of deep relaxation. Embody an expanding sense of equanimity and reflection. Connect to and integrate a greater sense of well-being—a growing wholeness of self. Acknowledge and honor the time and energy you have dedicated to this mindfulness practice: Body Scan. Affirm the space you have just held sacred and the effort you have made to integrate mindfulness into your very being, naturally cultivating teaching from the heart of mindfulness. And when you are ready, gently open your eyes, greeting the world from a deeper place of reflection, of greater spaciousness of mind and expansiveness of heart.

In the process of the ongoing education of teachers, the essential moment is that of critical reflection on one's practice.

—Paulo Freire

Mindful Teaching

Still water reflects a clearer reality just as a still mind more clearly reflects the unfolding present moment. Reflection is the essence of further insight and growth, leading to sharper discernment and deeper wisdom.

Fifteen-year-old Jae Hoon was very proud of speaking English, and he was the first in his Korean family to do so. After three years in an English-speaking environment, he was confident in his abilities. However, his fellow students, friends, and teachers usually did not understand what he was trying to say. There was no doubt that Jae Hoon would continue in his progress; however, he didn't understand why he had to continue receiving English support. My classroom challenge was to help Jae Hoon, like many students gaining English proficiency, reach the next stage in his second-language learning.

Jae Hoon was completely unaware of the persistent mistakes he made when speaking and writing. He showed no recognition of what was correct or incorrect. Even when corrections were pointed out to him, he would indicate a vague acknowledgement but then plow on ahead, continually making the same mistakes over and over again. It seemed that this stage in Jae Hoo1n's second-language acquisition was taking forever, and he was getting upset and confused by continuing English support services. I searched desperately for a strategy to get Jae Hoon to the next stage in his language development.

Essentially, I wanted Jae Hoon to foster reflection as a skill, so reflection became the mindfulness quality to intentionally integrate into my strategy. I wanted to find a way to make Jae Hoon aware of his language use in order for him to channel his energy, not mine, into correcting his mistakes. I hoped that by building an awareness of what he was saying, he would build his inner ability to realize that something was a mistake in the first place. Then he could make needed corrections and find the motivation to take responsibility for his own learning.

My classroom teaching strategy was to focus on error correction in a secure environment, without embarrassment or anxiety. When Jae Hoon made a mistake while speaking, I would repeat what he said and then pause right before the error. Jae Hoon would then repeat the sentence, and when he got to the pause in the sentence it was his responsibility to figure out what didn't sound right and then correct it. In his writing, I would put a mark beside the line where a correction was needed, or two marks if there were two mistakes, and so on. Jae Hoon had to figure out what the mistakes were and then correct them himself.

Each time that Jae Hoon had to repeat an incorrect sentence, he had to remember to stop and think about what he needed to say, and then say it correctly. After repeated practice, I only had to give Jae Hoon a subtle look and he knew something needed correcting in his speech. Then he took the initiative to think back on what he had just said, repeat it carefully, and attempt to self-correct. In his writing, Jae Hoon had to stop, reflect, and realize what needed revision. This was a first step in establishing his awareness. This forced him to look more objectively at his work, build up his own inner criteria of what constituted correctness, and then take responsibility for self-correction.

Finding a classroom teaching strategy that built up Jae Hoon's own inner criteria was a powerful step to enable him to better discern his language usage. Through the skill of reflection, he unconsciously mobilized his will to take the necessary action. This powerful impact on student learning proved to be the crucial step in speeding his language acquisition and, subsequently, reaching his goal of no longer needing English support services.

The ability to self-reflect acted like a mirror into areas of my own life. How many things am I unaware of? How many times do hints abound that are glaringly obvious to others but not to me? In which areas of my life do I need deeper self-reflection? Do I pause so that space is made for greater discernment and clarity? The deep stillness of tranquility surfaces as a mirror reflection, inviting deeper wisdom to emerge.

✿ 6 ✿
SURRRENDER

*When the grass has been burnt by the fire of the steppe,
it will grow anew in summer.*

—MONGOLIAN PROVERB

✸ *Mindfulness Practice*

CHOOSE A FLAT SURFACE WHERE YOU CAN LIE
DOWN COMFORTABLY. In today's practice, Total Body
Relaxation, you are invited into a total relaxation of
mind and body. Check that there is no stress being
placed anywhere in the body. You may want to use a
hand towel to support your neck in order to prevent
any hyperextension, or place a small pillow under the
lower back or knees if necessary. Add any additional
pillows, even under the hands, to add a greater sense

of comfort anywhere the body may be seeking it. Now let the feet drop to each side and stretch out the arms away from the trunk of the body. Palms of the hands are facing up. Make any final adjustments as you invite the body to totally surrender into a place of deep comfort and ease, emotionally and physically preparing the space for this surrendering of self. Mentally say to yourself that you will remain awake; however, if you do fall asleep, know that you will still gain benefits from the mindfulness practice: Total Body Relaxation.

Begin by guiding your attention to soften and relax the face area. Let the tip of the tongue lightly touch the roof of the mouth so that the jaw is open and relaxed. Your cheeks, forehead, chin, eyes, and the entire face, are all surrendering and the entire body is sinking into relaxation. Your body welcomes this invitation to surrender into a conscious relaxation. Prepare to take three deep breaths and stretch the body three times. First stretch your entire body. Let the stretch originate from the very core of your belly. Extend the energy out through the limbs to reach your hands, feet, and the top of the head. Let this full body stretch sink the body into a deeper surrender. Now stretch the body again and, as you exhale with a long sigh, feel the entire body soften. On the third and final stretch, release your body to the floor and feel a wave of relaxation, a soothing, calming flow throughout your body.

As the body surrenders, so too, invite the breath to do the same. Feel the breath gradually reduce in strength until it reaches a smooth, steady flow: gently, slowly, naturally becoming less and less perceptible. Rest in this place of deeper and deeper relaxation. Rest in this place of deeper and deeper surrender, and enjoy the next several minutes of total body relaxation.

Remain in this relaxed position, and when you are ready, bring gentle awareness to your breath and body; notice, too, your state of mind. You may sense the mind has also surrendered. The mind craves a sense of spaciousness, of no-thought, a place of deep peace and well-being. Surrendering first the physical body encourages the breath to calm the mind until it, too, finds the proper conditions for thoughts to lessen. When the mind has a resting place, even as it is still conscious, a profound sense of renewal and joyful ease of being are rewarded to both mind and body. The stresses of daily life fall away, soothing the nerves, releasing fatigue and stress. Total Body Relaxation, total surrender, no doing, no trying, no thinking.

SINK INTO THIS SURRENDERING AND CONTEM-
PLATE THE IDEA OF SURRENDER. Is your body
always on the go? Is there always something on your
mind? Are there times when surrendering would be
beneficial? Do certain choices you make tend to acti-
vate mind and body? Do they increase stress on the
nervous system? Or do you tend to seek out a sense
of renewal, nourishing a more interior part of your
being? Can surrendering become a friendly ally in
cultivating mindfulness throughout a busy day?

WITH A LONG, DEEP INHALE, DRAW IN THE
BREATH FROM YOUR BELLY, and as you exhale send
its energy to the extremities of your body. Bring in
another full, deep breath and stretch out your arms
and legs with a sense of newness, with light and love
reaching every cell of your body. Take another stretch,
this time wiggling your toes and fingers awake. Sense
a deep vitality and renewal of both mind and body
fill your being. This practice may appear easy but is
actually one of the most challenging of all: total surrender. Surrender of the body is only possible when it
has found total ease, and surrender of the mind is only
possible when the breath stills and thoughts dissipate
into ether.

EXTERNALIZE THE SENSES BY BECOMING MORE AWARE OF THE SOUNDS AROUND YOU. Breathe in the space to enjoy this moment, a pause from the inner to the outer, integrating the two as one. Embody this deep sense of well-being that surrendering has brought through today's mindfulness practice: Total Body Relaxation. Honor the time and energy you have dedicated to this practice. Affirm the space you have just held sacred and the effort you have made to integrate mindfulness into your very being, naturally cultivating teaching from the heart of mindfulness. And when you are ready, gently open your eyes, greeting the world from a deeper place of surrender, of greater spaciousness of mind and expansiveness of heart.

The subordination of teaching to learning is the only way of handling the challenge of freeing students while ensuring that they learn by an economic exchange of their time for a maximum of learning.

—CALEB GATTEGNO

Mindful Teaching

Surrendering is giving in wholeheartedly to what is present. When we battle against something, there is resistance, and energy is not fluid. Yet when we do surrender, our life-force becomes positive, opening to a greater wholeness of self.

Pierre was a delightful boy who, by the age of three, had four primary caregivers. Each interacted with Pierre in their own mother tongue: biological dad in French, mom in German, stepdad in English, and the nanny in Hindi. Beginning in kindergarten, Pierre had been enrolled in an American school in which English was the language of instruction. By the end of that year, English had become his dominant language, both socially and academically. I first started teaching Pierre English as an Additional Language when he entered grade four.

Though Pierre's progress may have been slower than that of a student with a similar background in several languages, it was unusual that he still hadn't produced one fluid sentence beyond basic language needs. For instance, he could easily talk about daily tasks and routines, or converse about his likes and dislikes. However, he would hesitate or repeat half a sentence several times when he attempted to express something more complicated (i.e., higher-order thinking or academic cognitive language), such as describing one of his favorite soccer players in a recent match or the way the moon rotates around the Earth. Classmates and teachers had a hard time understanding him. In similar cases, with further English-language immersion and English support services, students become fluent, which includes acquiring academic English at grade level. I assumed that Pierre would, over the course of the school year, achieve these goals. That was both my hope and classroom challenge. However, after the first few months of school, my doubts grew. Eventually, Pierre was tested for learning needs and was diagnosed with certain labels that kept changing over time. He received individualized learning services and private occupational therapy sessions to support his learning and development. Specialists, administrators, and classroom teachers all lowered their school expectations for Pierre. I, on the other hand, still believed that, given optimal learning conditions, Pierre was capable of reaching grade-level academic standards.

Although I didn't lose sight of the goal for Pierre to achieve a higher proficiency level in English, I knew that it was equally important—and the major component of my intentional mindfulness quality—to surrender to the circumstances. This meant for me to become more comfortable with Pierre's current abilities and provide the conditions for him to achieve success at his own rate, in his own time.

Communicating a sense of success in what Pierre had already achieved was a good starting point. This supports the basic teaching principle of accepting the student exactly where they are, but I recognized that, in this instance, I had not yet done so. Therefore, accepting Pierre's language abilities at their current levels was my act of surrender. Once I had done so, I put my plan in place, following two simple classroom teaching strategies: provide an environment that is language-rich and create an atmosphere conducive to a sense of well-being. Another essential strategy was working in partnership with Pierre's parents, teachers, and administrators. Specifically, I wanted to design an Individualized Educational Plan that we could all implement as a collaborative team.

After getting this plan in place, Pierre initiated a project that incorporated oral and written expression and one in which his social and leadership skills played a big role. Pierre created a news program of which he was the producer and anchorman and had a staff of fellow classmates on special assignments. He chose the topics, assigned research to each member of the group, and wrote and edited different scripts to read. He also orchestrated the presentation of the news program to other students, teachers, and his parents.

The entire process of producing the news program built up Pierre's language skills, and there was significant student learning in the areas of listening, speaking, reading, writing, and higher-order thinking skills in English. By constantly rehearsing English in written and oral form, Pierre showed a newfound confidence. There was a dramatic improvement in English skills by the time his news program went live. Meanwhile his cheerful disposition continued to flourish. Pierre presented more news programs throughout the remainder of the school year, and his abilities in self-expression grew with each presentation. By year's end, much to everyone's delight, Pierre eventually reached fluent English proficiency levels. This was a great achievement for Pierre and one of which he was extremely proud. Allowing Pierre to be Pierre helped him to become fluent in at least one language, and his self-esteem grew exponentially—two attributes that would benefit him throughout life.

Pierre helped me to face my challenges with less struggle and to slow down. Slowing down inevitably cultivates a greater appreciation of the present. Upon further self-reflection, by surrendering to what is, I can better see what I can or cannot do. Accepting with grace those things I cannot change gives me the freedom to discover what positive things I can bring to bear on a situation. Thus, depleting, stressful energy transforms into positive, self-renewing energy, and the act of surrendering opens a fuller presence of being and more space for the heart to receive.

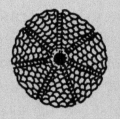

❈7❈
DETACHMENT

We cannot see things in perspective until we cease to hug
them to our own bosom. When we begin to let go of them
we begin to appreciate them as they really are.

—THOMAS MERTON

 *Mindfulness Practice*

COME INTO A COMFORTABLE SEATED POSITION.
Rest the palms of each hand on your thighs or place
them palms-up in your lap, and gently close your eyes.
Take a moment to sense how a straight spine and
open heart encourage a relaxed but alert pose. When
you are ready, bring awareness to a full cycle of breathing: a complete in-breath and a complete out-breath.
Continue as you bring an ever-increasing awareness

to the breath. Feel a growing sense of calm and invite in a spaciousness of mind and an expansiveness of heart as you transition into today's mindfulness practice: Recollecting.

WITH EVER-INCREASING FOCUS OF ATTENTION ON THE IN-BREATH AND THE OUT-BREATH, observe your body and its sensations. Continue in this practice until your mind has gently rested into the inhalation and exhalation of a slower, smoother, calmer breath. Inhale and exhale, inhale and exhale.

NOW BRING YOUR FOCUS OF ATTENTION ON THE PLACEMENT OF THE BREATH. Choose a point of contact where you can feel the incoming breath and the outgoing breath on the face. It may be at the base of the nostrils, the inner tip of the nostrils, or maybe just above the upper lip. Whichever spot you choose, let this be the point of concentration of breath awareness during the mindfulness practice of Recollecting. Settle into this focused attention on the breath; observe its incoming sensations and then its outgoing sensations. Keep the mind watchful and observant, not changing anything, building a witnessing awareness of the breath. Breathe in and breathe out, breathe in and breathe out.

THE NEXT TIME YOUR FOCUS OF ATTENTION WANDERS FROM THE BREATH and before you redirect your focus back to the breath, notice what arises. When you observe what arises, it will be one of the five kinds of sense perception—Hearing, Touching, Smelling, Seeing, Tasting, or it will be the last category of recollecting, Thinking, in which case you are using your imagination. For example, if you hear a sound: Hearing. Or if you notice your fingers against your clothes: Touching. This is the practice of recollecting what arises when the mind wanders from the breath, which it will inevitably do. When it does, simply recollect and then go back to the breath to the point of contact of the inhalation and exhalation: breathe in and breathe out, and stay focused on the breath. Continue with the breath; when another thought arises, one that, for instance, comes from your imagination, take note: Thinking. Then gently welcome back breath awareness, continue to observe the point of contact of the inhalation and exhalation. Inhalation of the in-breath, exhalation of the out-breath. When the focus of attention or awareness wanders the next time, observe and recollect again.

THERE IS NO JUDGMENT; RECOLLECTING IS A NEUTRAL OBSERVATION: Thinking, Hearing, Touching, Smelling, Seeing, or Tasting. Recollect and then redirect the focus of attention back to the breath. Watch the breath. Feel the breath on the point of contact of the inhalation and exhalation. Breathe in and out, inhale and exhale. A wandering thought: Thinking, Hearing, Touching, Smelling, Seeing, or Tasting. Now back to the breath, continuing in the mindfulness practice of Recollecting. Stay with the breath, and when thoughts or sensations arise again, recollect. Notice, observe, recollect, and simultaneously let whatever arises dissolve as attention is brought back to the breath. Breathe in and breathe out, breathe in and breathe out.

THIS MINDFULNESS PRACTICE IN THE ART OF RECOLLECTING CULTIVATES A CALMER, MORE SERENE, AND MORE HARMONIOUS BALANCE. Rest in this place of growing relaxation and deeper well-being—a recollection of your truer nature within. Enjoy this moment, a pause from the inner to the outer, integrating the two as one. A degree of detachment, in the abiding space of recollecting, can be a skillful means to navigate toward a wholeness of being. When you find yourself facing challenging situations, do so from a place of detachment with the knowledge that they, too, like arising thoughts and sensations, will pass.

WHEN YOU ARE READY TO TRANSITION OUT OF THE PRACTICE, LET GO OF THE FOCUS OF ATTENTION ON THE BREATH. Begin to externalize the senses by becoming more aware of the sounds around you. Enjoy this moment of greater equanimity and calm detachment. Acknowledge and honor the time and energy you have dedicated to today's mindfulness practice: Recollecting. Affirm the space you have just held sacred and the effort you have made to integrate mindfulness into your very being, naturally cultivating teaching from the heart of mindfulness. And when you are ready, gently open your eyes. With a growing detachment from thoughts and sensations and a recollection of your truer nature within, greet the world with a greater spaciousness of mind and expansiveness of heart.

Letting go of judgments does not mean ignoring errors. It simply means seeing events as they are and not adding anything to them.

—W. Timothy Gallwey

Mindful Teaching

Although detachment implies a separation from one's surroundings, it helps magnify reality with greater clarity. Detachment is an essential aspect of any mindfulness practice. To retreat into meditation, contemplation, or prayer invites in a detachment that touches the essence of truth.

One summer I was part of the faculty in a Master of Arts in Teaching program in southern Vermont. My class comprised graduate students who were experienced teachers from around the world. Just as I try to do in all my classes, I put much care and thought into creating a reflective and trusting classroom environment from the very first day onward. Students were attentive listeners, and everyone's contribution was honored. By the middle of the course, a strong community of learners had been established. Then I began to observe that Julia, previously one of the most actively involved and vocal students, offered her opinions and feedback less and less until she did so only sporadically. As I continued to observe her more closely, I noticed her withdrawing even further from class discussions and interactions. After several more classes, I decided to approach Julia and inquire about this change. However, she was not ready or willing to talk about it or share any reason for her change of attitude. Since I did not gain any helpful insights from Julia, I questioned whether she was progressing as a learner and whether I was responding effectively as a teacher. Julia continued to submit required work and written assignments. However, since I assess learning largely during class discussion, I found myself anxiously questioning how much learning was actually occurring in class. I also wondered whether I should be intervening in a different way. This overall situation was one of concern and one that I considered a classroom challenge.

By analyzing the situation from a distance, I saw clearly that I had begun to feel personally responsible for how Julia was choosing whether or not to participate in class. At this point, I realized that I did not need to take ownership of Julia's choices. My primary goal was to serve as a vehicle to facilitate learning and professional growth for Julia, and not just for Julia, but for all the course participants. I assessed that I had done my best to be sensitive to Julia's individual learning style, personality, and behavior. I sensed detachment would be a helpful quality to call upon in this situation, and so detachment became the intentional mindfulness quality with which to address this classroom challenge.

Respecting and protecting a more passive role for a student is not a typical classroom teaching strategy, yet it was the one I implemented in this scenario. I stopped designing activities that put Julia in active participatory roles; for instance, in group work or team collaboration she took on the more passive roles, such as recorder or timer for the group. I stopped directly asking Julia questions in class, and if a student did so, I would allow time for Julia to decide whether to answer or not, and if not, I would redirect the question and invite another student to respond. Instances like this allowed Julia simply to be present in class without pressure of participation. I had to trust that what I was doing was providing the most effective learning environment for Julia.

After another month, the class came to an end. Julia passed the course, but I never really knew the degree of her learning until after the final evaluation. That's when Julia came to my office to meet with me in order to express her appreciation. We had a brief conversation in which Julia shared that she had learned a lot, both at an educational and personal level. She also commented that unexpected personal issues caused her tremendous stress and worry over the course of the summer. As Julia left my office, she commented, "Although it was too hard for me to share my personal situation, I now realize how much it affected me in class. There were so many times I almost burst out in tears. Your silent support sustained me through the worst time. I was ready to quit and withdraw from the program, but knowing that I could just show up to class without pressure to talk helped me make it through the course. And I feel I have learned so much and grown as a teacher." I was very thankful for Julia's visit and the ensuing conversation. It confirmed that the strategies I'd employed had a positive impact on Julia's learning, something I may never have known otherwise.

I had been so wrapped up in feeling responsible for Julia and her learning that I had weighed myself down with searching for a solution. Once I had detached myself, I was released from the net

I had created. Julia breathed more easily, learning occurred, and resolution was reached.

Julia's example helped me reflect that, as a teacher, I have a primary responsibility to create an effective learning environment. At times, this can mean that a certain degree of detachment from feeling overly responsible for each student is not only helpful, but vital. It was only after I detached myself from the entanglement of the situation that I saw how wrapped up I had become. Detachment created the space that allowed me to see more clearly. Detachment gave me room to breathe. Detachment helped calm my thoughts so I could see with greater clarity. With clarity came wiser action.

The ability to detach myself from difficult classroom challenges has helped me become better equipped to enhance student learning and bring renewed energy to my teaching. Through self-reflection, I understand how practicing detachment in the classroom has also helped me build detachment as a useful skill when dealing with life's challenges, such as raising teenagers, juggling many responsibilities, or facing times of crisis. Attaining a certain sense of detachment from day-to-day life helps us better connect to the wellspring of an interior life and its spiritual nature.

❀8❀
PERSEVERANCE

The power of intelligence can set meadows afire,
but perseverance can wear away a stone.

TIBETAN PROVERB

🌼 *Mindfulness Practice*

COME INTO A COMFORTABLE SEATED POSI-
TION. Rest the palms of each hand on your thighs
or upturned in your lap and gently close your eyes.
Mentally review your posture, especially the strength
of your base and the alignment of your spine. Make
any adjustments and feel a natural lengthening of your
entire body as the crown of the head reaches sky-
ward and the heart opens in all directions. When you
are ready, bring awareness to a full cycle of breath-

ing: a complete in-breath and a complete out-breath. Continue as you bring an ever-increasing awareness to the breath. Feel a growing sense of calm as you transition into today's mindfulness practice: Labeling—Past, Present, Future.

WITH EVER-INCREASING FOCUS OF ATTENTION ON THE IN-BREATH AND THE OUT-BREATH, continue to watch the breath. Sense the moment the inhalation starts and the moment the inhalation ends. Sense the moment the exhalation starts and the moment the exhalation ends. Continue in this practice until you feel that your awareness has gently rested into the inhalation and exhalation of an increasingly slower, smoother, calmer breath. Inhale and exhale, inhale and exhale.

THE NEXT TIME YOUR FOCUS OF ATTENTION WANDERS FROM THE BREATH, and before bringing your awareness back to the breath, first notice that the attention is elsewhere. Then, before redirecting awareness back to the breath, observe, take note, and label the thought; it is either a thought about the past, present, or future. If it is about remembering something that has already happened, simply label it: Past. For example, "I loved the mountain scene in the book I was reading last night. It reminded me of last summer's hike in the green mountains in Vermont. I had so much fun that day . . ." Then redirect your awareness back to the breath. Inhale and exhale and stay focused on the breath. A thought: "I am aware that I am feeling cool air coming in at the base of the nostril as I am inhaling right now." Its label: Present. Continue with the breath. Then another thought comes to mind: "Ah, I am thinking about what I need to do once I finish this practice. I don't want to forget to pick up the things I need for dinner tonight." Its label: Future. Then gently welcome the attention back to breath awareness. Continue observing the beginning point and ending point of each inhalation and each exhalation. Inhalation of the in-breath, exhalation of the out-breath.

WHEN THE MIND WANDERS OFF AGAIN, OBSERVE THE THOUGHT and note whether it is Past, Present, or Future. No judgment. A neutral observation: Past, Present, or Future. Then redirect the focus of attention back to the breath. Watch the breath. Feel the breath, in, out, inhaling, exhaling, air coming in through the nose, out through the nose, air rising in the lungs and belly, belly and lungs releasing. An incoming thought arriving, noticing, labeling: Past, Present, or Future. Back to the breath. Stay with the breath. When another thought comes, label it, and as you do so the thought dissolves on its own as attention is brought back to the breath. Now continue in the mindfulness practice of Labeling—Past, Present, Future.

WHEN YOU FIND YOUR PRACTICE REACHING A CALMER, MORE SERENE SPACE, REST IN THIS PLACE. Sense a deeper well-being, greater wholeness, and increased mindfulness. Thoughts coming, thoughts going, noticing, observing, labeling. Not being drawn into the past or pulled into the future but grounded in the spaciousness of the moment. A growing sense of wellness, a growing sense of calm and relaxation. A growing sense of skillful mindfulness as you watch thoughts come and go while staying grounded in the breath. Grounded in a growing inner stillness and calm, welcoming a degree of perseverance to stay grounded in this quiet awareness as thoughts come and go, aware but detached from their tug and pull. A spaciousness in which an expansiveness of mind and heart are encouraged to blossom and take hold. Rest in this ease of being. Enjoy its ever-growing power in you. Relish this moment, a pause from the inner to the outer, integrating the two as one.

WHEN YOU ARE READY, INVITE THE BREATH BACK AS YOU PREPARE TO EXTERNALIZE THE SENSES. From a place of relaxation and calm detachment, integrate a greater sense of wholeness. Take a fuller in-breath and a fuller out-breath. Acknowledge and honor the time and energy you have dedicated to today's mindfulness practice: Labeling—Past, Present, Future. Affirm the space you have just held sacred and the effort you have made to integrate mindfulness into your very being, naturally cultivating teaching from the heart of mindfulness. And when you are ready, gently open your eyes, knowing that perseverance in the practices helps you to greet the world from a deeper place of wholeness, of greater spaciousness of mind and expansiveness of heart.

It does not matter how slowly you go as long as you do not stop.

—CONFUCIUS

Mindful Teaching

When starting out on the journey we can be filled with enthusiasm to reach the goal, yet challenging trials and tribulations abound along the path. Courage and sheer willpower can also help overcome challenges; but eventually it is perseverance that is needed in order to keep on keeping on. Perseverance can be the ultimate challenge in reaching the next step, leading to further insights and transformation.

Ariel was one of those students I had heard about long before she entered my class in grade five. Every teacher who had worked with her since first grade had a similar story: "Ariel will be delightful for the first few weeks, but over time things will change. She'll become moody and manipulative. She won't stay on task. She won't complete her homework. She'll only do things on her own terms. She'll end up having a personality conflict with you and all her teachers. It is easier just to let her do what she wants; otherwise, she'll drive you crazy!" After hearing these dramatic admonitions, my classroom challenges were defined even before the first day of class: for me to have a productive relationship with Ariel and for Ariel to have a successful learning experience.

Ariel's first two weeks of the school year matched the description of my colleagues: Ariel was cheerful, motivated to improve her skills, and fun to have in class. Heeding the warnings of her former teachers, I thought the best strategy would be to put Ariel in charge of her own learning. Responsibility for decision making would rest squarely on her shoulders. This would help Ariel feel in charge. I also hoped it would avoid future conflicts with me. In order to put this plan in place in the very first week, I asked Ariel to think about three of her classroom expectations. By the end of the second week, Ariel had her three ideas. I explained what a contract is and I suggested we write up a teacher-student contract of our own. I made a big deal out of it in order to build up her sense of pride and importance in both deciding on the content and being a signatory on such an important document. Basically, I was trying to stress the importance of this "binding" agreement and her to decision to abide by it. By the end of the third week, we wrote up her three expectations in the form of a contract, and then we both signed it. Specifically, Ariel agreed that she would: 1) Complete and submit legible homework on time; 2) Stay on task in class; and 3) Continue trying her best even when she was moody. Now that I had been proactive in setting up a situation that would contribute to Ariel's success, I was determined to see it through and stay steady for the year ahead. My classroom teaching strategy was to stick to the contract and not waver on the three expectations. They were doable and within reach, and they would encourage positive learning habits. My very intentional mindfulness quality was to have the perseverance to stay the course!

In the first few weeks after the contract was signed, Ariel grew to see me as a person who was looking out for her, and trust was beginning to grow between us. Things seemed to be moving in the right direction. I thought, "How easy! I have this situation figured out!" Then slowly and almost imperceptibly, for no apparent reason, Ariel began to change. A few more weeks passed as Ariel's behavior seemed less positive; she did not stay on task as much, and she became somewhat moody. By the end of the second month, I found myself in the same situation as Ariel's previous teachers: evidently she decided she didn't want to work anymore. Her homework became less and less legible until it was hard to decipher, and by the end of the third month she stopped handing in homework altogether. Even though I would sit down with Ariel and ask how she was doing and then remind her of the contract, she would find a justification for everything. Now into the second quarter, Ariel was rarely on task, she got moodier by the day, and she told me that henceforth she would no longer honor our "contract" or work toward the goals she had previously agreed to. Though at wits' end, I was determined not to give up.

Ariel's unwillingness to take responsibility for her decisions and her actions astounded me. Unlike her previous teachers, though, I continued to hold her accountable to the expectations she had set, just as we had originally agreed. I still believed that persevering in following the contract was the right thing to do. When Ariel sensed that I was sticking by our contract, her moodiness and manipulation and other adverse behavior escalated. She would skip class by going to the guidance counselor, without prior permission or knowledge from any teacher. When Ariel was in class, she oftentimes threw temper tantrums. To make matters worse, she left teary-eyed, complaining to other teachers and administrators.

In my heart of hearts, I felt that the mindfulness quality, perseverance, was exactly what was needed to best serve Ariel. She had the skills necessary to accomplish the goals she had set, and she had displayed the courage and self-determination to try to reach them in those first few weeks. At the same time, even after over twenty years of teaching, I seriously questioned my professional ability. I even wondered if Ariel was purposefully going out of her way to threaten my professional standing. Despite these self-doubts, I still felt the best way was to forge ahead in my resolve rather than give in and perpetuate the situation, as Ariel's previous teachers had done. I decided that no matter what Ariel said, or however hard she campaigned to sabotage my credibility, I was going to stick to our agreement and persevere.

My strategy didn't produce immediate results: Ariel didn't change. As her negative behavior continued, I realized that I needed to advocate for my decisions beyond the classroom and enlist the support of a team. This first meant going to my immediate supervisor and a few other key administrators and counselors to explain the situation, describe Ariel's behavior, and articulate my reasons for sticking to the contract. I spoke to all of Ariel's current teachers, telling them the same. I met with Ariel's parents, who had always been supportive but were also nearing wits' end with Ariel themselves. I gained immediate support from all of them and, much to my delight, a large degree of empathy as well. This was a tremendous help in feeling more secure in the decision I had made. Their support better equipped me to persevere with the strategy I had outlined with Ariel. As a boon, gaining institutional support removed any doubts about my professional standing.

Ariel continued with her moody outbursts and cried more fiercely than before. She freely expressed her disdain for me in front of other students in class. This continued for the entire second quarter, surely putting student learning at jeopardy. By the time winter break came, little had changed. I spent that vacation with a nagging sense of dread and doubt. Had I made the right decision? Will my strategy help or hinder Ariel? Have I put myself in a dire situation? What will happen when school reopens?

With the advent of the new year and the return to school, I received Ariel in warmth and kindness. I also had renewed energy that clearly communicated my belief that Ariel could meet her stated goals. Although Ariel tested her boundaries that first week back at school by shouting and resisting school assignments, by the end of the second week her anger began to subside.

By the beginning of the next month back, Ariel showed subtle signs of compliance. She started to turn in legible homework that showed true effort. This was the first concrete sign of positive student learning. Then Ariel started being a willing participant in group activities. Another positive sign! By the end of the third quarter, Ariel began to express enthusiasm in group discussions. Her behavior kept improving, at first being sustained over several days and then over weeks at a time. By the time the last quarter of the school year approached, Ariel was taking initiative in her own learning, suggesting ways she could improve and then mapping out a game plan for reaching her goals. Her skills in all subject areas improved, as did her study skills both in and out of class. Ariel was friendlier with me and we reestablished the easygoing relationship that had flourished in those initial weeks of the school year. By the time fifth-grade graduation came, a strong foundation of trust and respect had been established between us. This foundation, which took a full school year to achieve, stood the test of time. The following year, when Ariel was on a break she would often come into my classes, always lending a helping hand to students and giving them encouragement.

Then from time to time all the way through her high school years, Ariel would pop into my class when I was working after school, confiding in me or asking advice on issues she was facing at school. In short, I had become one of Ariel's most trusted teachers.

Ariel and I had built a strong relationship based on mutual trust before I stuck to my zero-tolerance strategy with her. Intuitively, I was sure she knew that I believed in her, and I thought that this would sustain us through the rocky period that was so very trying. I'm glad that I didn't waver in my resolve and instead stayed the course to witness the positive outcome. It was very gratifying to see Ariel take responsibility, improve her skills, and meet new challenges. Upon self-reflection, I began to understand just how much perseverance I had mustered to face this classroom challenge, but at a certain point there seemed to be only one choice—forge ahead. I see how this taught me that perseverance, no matter what the odds, helps ensure that resolution is reached. One phase of the journey reaches completion so a new one can begin.

9
GRATITUDE

There are no mistakes, no coincidences.
All events are blessings given to us to learn from.

—ELISABETH KÜBLER-ROSS

Mindfulness Practice

COME INTO A COMFORTABLE SEATED POSITION.
Gently rest your hands on your thighs or place them
palms-up in your lap. Roll the tongue lightly so that
the jaw relaxes, and let your eyes close softly. As you
settle into a relaxed but engaged posture, invite in an
alert but calm mind. Bring awareness to a full cycle of
breathing: a complete in-breath and a complete out-
breath. With ever-increasing awareness of the breath,
feel a growing sense of calm as you transition into
today's mindfulness practice: Heartfulness.

WHEN YOU ARE READY, DIRECT THE FOCUS OF attention to the belly rising on the in-breath and falling on the out-breath. Concentrate your full awareness on this breathing and bring your mind back to the focus of attention whenever you notice it wandering. Belly rising on the inhalation, belly sinking in on the exhalation. Continue in this practice for several more minutes. As a growing calm envelops you, sit in its embrace. Then, with the softest of movements, gently bring your hands together in prayer position an inch or two in front of the middle of your upper chest, the heart chakra. The base of each palm touches the other and the tips of the thumbs and pinky fingers also touch each other. The three middle fingers—the index fingers, middle fingers, and ring fingers—open up and spread out. Both palms are open, and the fingertips spread outward. The gesture has become that of a lotus flower. Stay in this gesture as long as it feels comfortable. While holding it, continue to focus on the breath: belly rising on the in-breath and falling on the out-breath. Breathe in and breathe out, breathe in and breathe out, and continue in this practice.

FROM A PLACE OF CALM OBSERVATION, WITHOUT JUDGMENT, and witnessing from a place of equanimity, are there sensations or feelings that naturally emerge from holding the gesture of the lotus flower? Now let go of watching the breath and bring your attention, your witnessing self, to be in this open presence, holding the lotus flower in front of the heart. Be with what is. Observe. Feel. Witness. Perhaps the breath naturally lengthens and feels more expansive just as this gesture opens up to the unfolding nature of the heart. The inherent nature of the heart, a warmheartedness, one of unconditional love, unbound by time or space, not limited by thoughts or emotions—this is the unstuck nature of a loving heart: a boundless joy, a heartfelt expansion of life, unstuck from reactions, thoughts, or feelings of the mind, but emerging from a deep inner wisdom of your own true nature within.

WHILE HOLDING THE SHAPE OF THE LOTUS FLOWER, and with it the many facets of unconditional love, you can feel the gesture itself as various aspects of the lotus. Its base, stemming from within and growing out of a strong foundation shaped by the palms, little fingers, and thumbs touching, holding the form. A receptacle holding the space, a sense of receiving and giving at the same time. A vessel, one strong enough to hold the unfolding space of lightness. A blossoming flower that has grown in strength through courage, acceptance, compassion, perseverance, and other qualities of a healing nature. This inner strength unfolds into the present moment, bringing with it deep gratitude, an ability to face whatever has emerged—without fear, rejection, clinging, or avoidance. Recognize that a deeper inner wisdom has brought whatever is necessary to this present moment, with heartfelt gratitude, one of total acceptance and understanding. Feel the present moment as a true blessing. With this heartfelt gratitude, the open space of the lotus flower contains a love so strong that it keeps unfolding without end. A source of abundance blossoming forth from a loving heart. A grace of being in the present moment. A heart so full that all is forgiven, all is embraced because all is connected in love.

INVITE IN A PRESENT-MOMENT AWARENESS from an unfolding heart, connected to all, and one that is expansive and healing in nature. Mindfulness can always be brought back to the heart, inviting in a feeling away from the head and to the true place where inner wisdom resides. With a present-moment awareness, embody this experience: deep gratitude, grace, abundance, a loving heart. Dedicate this heartfulness, from an open presence of a quiet, spacious mind to the seat of inner wisdom of a loving heart, to any person or situation you feel may benefit. Know that this dedication makes a difference, for it is accompanied by a grace and beauty of heartfulness and the abundant nature of love, touching and healing all it embraces.

WHEN YOU ARE READY, RELEASE THE GESTURE of the lotus flower, and let your hands rest on your thighs or place them in your lap. Invite back awareness to the breath: inhale and exhale, inhale and exhale. Embody and integrate gratitude and abundance into a loving heart. Enjoy this moment, a pause from the inner to the outer, integrating the two as one. Now, with slightly more awareness of the breath as you prepare to externalize the senses, take a fuller in-breath and a fuller out-breath. Acknowledge and honor the time and energy you have dedicated to this mindfulness practice: Heartfulness. Integrate this increased sense of wholeness—a wholeness filled with grace and thanksgiving. Affirm the space you have just held sacred and the effort you have made to integrate mindfulness into your very being, naturally cultivating teaching from the heart of mindfulness. And when you are ready, gently open your eyes, greeting the world from a deeper place of gratitude, of greater spaciousness of mind and expansiveness of heart.

When you are grateful fear disappears and abundance appears.

—ANTHONY ROBBINS

Mindful Teaching

True gratitude is a humbling of the sacredness within, embracing and celebrating the abundance that has been showered upon us. Gratitude is a melting of the heart center, shedding the protective layers of fear and, in turn, unlocking a free flow of love and its transformative healing powers.

Feeling awkward and uncomfortable in the class-room is normal for a new student, especially when they enter after the school year has begun. This is particularly accentuated when the student doesn't speak the common language of the school community. Ari was just such a student. He had loved going to school in his home country of Israel.

In his second-grade class he had been considered the smartest student and he had been popular and well liked.

For the first two weeks in his new school, Ari completely rejected the environment: he was mean to fellow students and rude to all his teachers; he didn't follow school rules; and he would have temper tantrums and throw things all over the classroom. His parents were concerned for Ari's transition and horrified to see their son exhibit such antisocial behavior. Even though I knew that in time and with the acquisition of English Ari would be fine, I wanted to feel grateful for having such a student in my class.

Although other mindfulness practices such as surrender, acceptance, or compassion are equally appropriate to call upon in such a situation, I chose to employ the lens of gratitude; specifically, to be happy that this student was placed in my class. Determining the classroom challenge was easy and straightforward: to ensure a positive transition into the new learning environment for Ari, and to do so as quickly as possible! However, the mindfulness quality I chose, gratitude, was more challenging. I wanted to connect to the feeling of gratitude when Ari was in class and when I was interacting directly with him. Though this sounds simple, I had to find the place inside myself, beyond just feeling and knowing it logically, but actually feeling gratitude from my heart.

My classroom teaching strategy was threefold: 1) Team up with Ari's parents to learn what subjects he liked, what subjects he excelled in, and what achievements he could share from his old school and show to his new class. 2) Design a plan for Ari to work in his areas of interest, both in his native language, Hebrew, and in English, and then to present a project to the class in English. Ari would receive lots of one-on-one attention and help in English in order for him to feel confident for his first presentation. 3) Coach the rest of the class, explaining why Ari behaved how he did and encourage them to be patient with him and try to be understanding, kind, and caring, no matter what behavior Ari displayed.

Surprisingly, when I could connect to a deep sense of gratitude, a different energy seemed to emerge. It felt like a sense of magic and grace were made tangible. I was completely open and caring in a deeply new and grateful way. It seemed that Ari could feel it, too, and that he also connected to this sense of thankfulness. It was a small connection, but one that grew over time. The first step was Ari feeling safe with me and in my class—his only safe haven for the first few months. I was able to communicate progress in Ari's improved behavior and outlook to other teachers; they, in turn, gave Ari a little more individual attention and positive encouragement.

Ari began to improve noticeably in his motivation, confidence, and skills, and student learning was immediately evident. Ari demonstrated great courage and determination to present, in English, his first project. It was well received by his fellow classmates, and I could detect a hint of a smile on his face. By the end of the first semester, Ari had made other presentations with growing confidence and greater English proficiency. He was smiling more and more and beginning to fit in. Ari's comfort level steadily increased, as did his proficiency in English and his general academic skills. By the end of the first school year, Ari was performing at grade level. By the end of the second year, he was a confident student, outperforming most of his classmates. He was a kind friend to all, and well liked by his classmates.

Ari had been defiant, unruly, uncontrollable, and angry when he first arrived. He had lost his grounding and had become fearful and deeply insecure. When I bring self-reflection to bear, I ask myself questions such as: How often do these same feelings manifest in me? Or how often do I, like Ari, lash out when I find myself in uncharted territory? How fearful am I? How inadequate do I feel? How often does my guard go up? How often do I build protective walls and close off my heart in the process? When am I blinded to the goodness in a difficult situation or person I am facing?

It's easy to face joyful occasions with gratitude. The true test is to be grateful during trying times. This is when gratitude and its abundant power of love can plunder the heart of all its fear. This depth of gratitude heals the heart, transforming the world through its grace.

❧10❧
JOYFUL HAPPINESS

By happiness I mean here a deep sense of
flourishing that arises from an exceptionally
healthy mind. This is not a mere pleasurable
feeling, a fleeting emotion, or a mood,
but an optimal state of being.

—MATTHIEU RICARD

Mindfulness Practice

COME INTO A COMFORTABLE SEATED POSI-
TION, and place your hands on your thighs or in
your lap. Stretch the top of your head a bit higher
and then tuck your chin in ever so slightly. This helps
lengthen the upper body and expand the chest area,
opening more space around the heart. Now relax your

face, close your eyes, and feel the outer creases of your eyes and mouth smile gently. Make any adjustments to feel a natural lengthening of your entire body and the heart opening in all directions. Bring awareness to a complete in-breath and a complete out-breath, and with ever-increasing awareness of the breath, invite in a growing sense of calm as you transition into today's mindfulness practice: Resting in the Heart.

Draw your attention to the middle of your body, at the solar plexus, just above the navel. Begin to draw in the breath, belly rising on the inhalation, belly falling on the exhalation. Continue to breathe like this until you feel your breath is calm and rhythmic. Breathe in and breathe out. Breathe in and breathe out. There may be a natural resting place at the solar plexus, a gap between the in-breath and out-breath. Whatever you notice, observe without changing anything. Breathe in and breathe out. Breathe in and breathe out. Continue, naturally breathing in and out, and when you feel a deep inner calm, mentally draw in the breath from the extremities of the body, from the head and the hands and the feet to the solar plexus. Try to feel or visualize this energy, the energy of the breath being drawn into the solar plexus. Trust whatever arises as the energy is drawn to the solar plexus. Absorb it there momentarily. Whether you're feeling this energy or visualizing it, sense it at the solar plexus, and on the exhalation send the energy out again to all the extremities of the body. Feel or visualize this energy nourishing the body as it is drawn back in again to the solar plexus and out again to the extremities. Guide this energy of the breath in a continuous rhythm of inhaling and exhaling. Breathe in and breathe out. Breathe in and breathe out.

As you continue, visualize your breath as energy streams of golden light. Imagine the golden light filling every cell of your body as the energy comes in on the inhaling breath and goes out on the exhaling breath. Feel the warmth of this golden light. Inhale and exhale. Breathe in and breathe out. Imagine the streams of golden light coming in from beyond your body, into your body from all sides, all the way to the solar plexus. Breathe in this warm, healing light, resting momentarily and absorbing its healing effects at the solar plexus, then let it penetrate every cell as you exhale it out to the body's extremities and beyond. Continue imagining this penetrating golden light.

On the next inhalation, direct the streams of golden light to the heart area. Let it bathe the heart and all it touches. Gather it there, and on the exhalation radiate it out through the body and as you do so, feel the warm, golden rays penetrate every cell. Stay with this golden light streaming in as it gathers at the heart on the inhalation and then expands outward on the exhalation. Continue to breathe in and out. You may feel a sense of greater expansion—inhaling, the golden light of breath opening you up; exhaling, this golden light of breath expanding you outward. With this ever-increasing opening up, there also comes the opportunity to integrate all that is—a joyful happiness of being. From a place of observation, witness any present-moment awareness of fleeting emotions or thoughts bathed in healing golden light, melting into a oneness of self, dissipating into the ether. With this integration, a sense of greater wholeness may emerge and begin to expand. Breathe in and breathe out, breathe in and breathe out.

REMAIN WITH YOUR EYES CLOSED AND MENTALLY PREPARE to bring your hands into the gesture of the heart. Gently place the right hand over the heart. Cup your palm so that a small space between your body and the palm invites the heart to breathe into this space. Place your left hand over the top of the right hand in a slightly crossed position so that your two hands receive your heart in a soft gesture, as if holding a most fragile gem. Continue to breathe in and out. Observe. Be aware of any sensations. Breathe in and out, in and out. Cultivate the boundless nature of the heart, the sacred privilege to hold your heart in its greater fullness. As the heart merges from this place of wholeness, you touch on the true nature of self, unbounded by time or space, unlimited by thoughts or emotions, emptied of grasping and clinging, of avoidance or rejection. This is the unstuck nature of the heart: a boundless joy of the ever-expanding present. This is joyful happiness, a heartfulness of being, a deep flourishing of self from an unfolding, loving heart, connected to all, one that is expansive and healing in nature.

AS YOU CONTINUE TO HOLD THIS GESTURE, ATTUNE TO THE MORE HARMONIOUS NATURE OF BEING that has been cultivated, an ever-expanding positive force that emerges from the heart. Let it penetrate into every cell of your body. This heartfulness of self is an essential seed of mindfulness: embody its essence. Though the thinking mind helps to skillfully build focus and attention, those are but tools to help open the gate where the essential nature of mindfulness—love, in its ever-expanding nature—lies in silent waiting. So when integrating mindfulness, cultivate this seed of mindfulness from a heartfulness of self.

WHEN YOU ARE READY, PREPARE TO TRANSI-
TION OUT OF THE PRACTICE and rest in this quiet
place, one of greater wholeness and well-being. Enjoy
this moment, a pause from the inner to the outer,
integrating the two as one. As you begin to externalize the senses, release the gesture and bring your
hands into prayer position. Acknowledge and honor
yourself and the time and energy you have dedicated
to this mindfulness practice: Resting in the Heart.
Integrate this increased sense of wholeness, its joyful happiness emerging from the heart. Affirm the
space you have just held sacred and the effort you
have made to integrate mindfulness into your very
being, naturally cultivating teaching from the heart
of mindfulness. And when you are ready, gently open
your eyes, greeting the world from a deeper place of
joyful happiness, of greater spaciousness of mind and
expansiveness of heart.

Happiness is when what you think, what you say, and what you do are in harmony.

—Mohandas Gandhi

Mindful Teaching

When joyful happiness bursts forth, its pure, effervescent nature merges with a universal oneness of love, healing oneself and others in the process. Moments of joyful happiness are precious celebrations of our inherent nature. How important it is to take time to rejoice, to hold these experiences dear as they sustain us and remind us of where we are headed!

A class made up of fifth-grade boys was relieved when their very strict and somewhat cranky teacher went on sick leave. They were even more delighted when they met the substitute: Diane, an enthusiastic woman in her early twenties. Her big smile and charismatic, welcoming personality combined to make her popular among her grade-five students. Although Diane had done some English teaching with preschoolers in South Korea and had tutored high school students during her undergraduate years in the United States, she had never received any kind of formal teacher training nor training in the subject area she was asked to teach, English as an Additional Language (EAL). Being fairly new to teaching, Diane was happy to get this job, albeit on a trial basis.

As Diane's mentor, I observed Diane thoroughly immerse herself in all classroom activities and exhibit a clear sense of deep involvement. She expressed to me how rewarding she found the interaction with her students and how happy she was to have this teaching opportunity. However, lacking any effective classroom-management style, the fifth graders were often seen fooling around in class, not caring about getting activities done or handing in homework. I suspected that these savvy students knew how to take advantage of Diane's goodwill and inexperience! Not only were the students off-task much of the time, but their unruly behavior left Diane exasperated. She told me that although she was trying her best to stay on top of the situation, she knew that effective student learning was being compromised. To make matters worse, she said she was totally overwhelmed and exhausted at the end of each school day.

Clearly, the classroom challenge was for Diane to become a competent EAL teacher. My aim was to help a fellow teacher develop the necessary skills, knowledge, and background in her subject area, EAL, and to use effective classroom-management techniques. I hoped that Diane would find her rhythm and flow and quickly establish a solid foundation as an effective teacher. Since a deep sense of joyful happiness was the bedrock of Diane's personality, I wanted to be sure to celebrate this sense of joy throughout the process. In order to ensure that this happiness would continue to express itself, I intentionally chose to focus on joyful happiness as the mindfulness quality.

In collaboration with Diane, we articulated several professional goals to meet. Guiding Diane to meet these goals became my classroom challenge. First, we sat down and mapped out a plan with detailed resources and learning opportunities to build Diane's understanding and expertise in EAL. We reviewed EAL skills and assessment benchmarks and how to plan lessons accordingly. We also drew up a schedule that gave Diane the opportunity to see effective classroom management in action by observing fellow teachers. In addition, we discussed the principles and practices of classroom management that she wanted to implement. We agreed to meet on a daily basis for immediate feedback and reflection during the first few weeks. We had quickly established a trusting and supportive rapport, and Diane had easy access to seek out my advice or expertise on an as-needed basis during school hours and beyond.

In just a few short weeks, Diane demonstrated significant professional growth by successfully implementing many of the strategies we had mapped out. Diane familiarized herself with EAL benchmarks in different skill areas and could design solid lesson plans to reach set goals. When introducing classroom activities and detailing specific learning goals she gave clear instructions, both orally and with visual tools. Diane, along with her students, came up with classroom agreements that included expected behavior, and this helped to further establish a community of learners based on mutual trust and respect. Diane was more proactive than reactive when dealing with student behavior, and students had much clearer expectations and support. All these improvements occurred while Diane continued to foster a warm, friendly classroom environment. Now the students were able to stay more on task, and this in turn had a positive impact that reinforced Diane's teaching ability. Needless to say, Diane was no longer overwhelmed or exhausted, and her enthusiasm kept on growing. By the second month, there was clear evidence of student progress in reaching EAL language benchmarks in all skill areas. Diane continued to witness her own effective teaching and her students' learning steadily grow on a daily basis. This further built her confidence and sense of success, and the classroom became a place of great joy and effective student learning. As a result, after the substitution job ended, Diane was hired on a full-time basis for the rest of that school year.

Diane experienced a range of emotions and faced many hurdles as that school year progressed. There were days when she needed courage or perseverance to succeed, and other days when she was mindful to integrate reflection or acceptance. Yet, steadily, I watched Diane's love for teaching take root. The most gratifying moment of all was when Diane expressed her joyful happiness to have found her passion for teaching. By spring she had applied to graduate school to become a certified teacher. Years later, Diane continues to share her love of teaching and finds the classroom a dynamic, gratifying environment, one in which I am sure her joyful happiness continues to express itself.

When I observed Diane in the classroom, she often seemed to be in a state of flow and she taught with a deep sense of joy. Her example propelled me to reflect on my own sense of joy and happiness. I read poems on these themes, reread books on positive psychology, and did some reading in texts from different traditions. That is when I learned that there is actually a word in Tibetan, *dekyi,* that means joyful happiness. I am very inspired to think that this concept, captured in one word, is part of the Tibetan worldview. For joyful happiness helps touch that sublime sense of our optimal state of being. Attaining this sense of joyful happiness is the reward for the mindful traveler who remains ever steady throughout the journey's challenges. It is a journey that calls on courage, compassion, reflection, and other mindfulness qualities. Looking back and reflecting on my own first steps in this journey, mindfulness has led me, step by step, to touch this essential nature of joyful happiness and cultivate its healing nature, more and more each day.

What lies behind us and what lies ahead of us are tiny matters compared to what lies within us.

—RALPH WALDO EMERSON

APPENDIX

HEARTS

A Mindfulness-Based Teaching Approach

Let the beauty we love be what we do.

—RUMI

Overview

THE HEARTS MINDFULNESS-BASED TEACHING APPROACH is based on the premise that all of life can be approached as a laboratory for practicing mindfulness. Translating this belief into action in the classroom through the HEARTS approach provides a pedagogical foundation that empowers teachers to be grounded in mindfulness and teaching practice. The HEARTS six-step protocol can be adapted to any subject, curriculum, or school setting. While this approach can be used on its own, it also complements any mindfulness-in-education initiative or mindfulness-based intervention. The acronym HEARTS serves as a reminder to teachers to stay anchored in the heartfelt nature at the core of mindfulness; at the same time, it equips teachers with a specific tool to cultivate more mindfulness in their daily lives, teaching lives, and in the lives of their students.

Following HEARTS provides a concrete tool that empowers you to experience this book interactively. You may be implementing the HEARTS mindfulness-based teaching approach individually in your own teaching context, in a peer-coaching forum, in a university course, or in another setting. However you adapt it, and whether you try out lessons based on the same themes in the book or discover creative alternatives, the choices you make help this become your personal journey in teaching from the heart of mindfulness.

The categories in HEARTS and their corresponding prompts serve as a roadmap for any mindfulness-based teaching approach. Writing the corresponding information under each heading, especially when first following the steps, reinforces a systematic methodology of reflecting on the process: articulating thoughts, provoking deeper insights, stimulating new ways of thinking, and assessing the journey. These prompts serve as springboards: you can follow them just as they are written, or you can write your own guiding questions that may speak more directly to you, or you can even change the acronym HEARTS to better capture your own journey. Once you feel grounded in a mindfulness-based teaching approach, a step-by-step process may not seem necessary at all.

A mindfulness quality, explained more fully in the following section, defines the guiding theme of this mindfulness-based teaching approach. Then follows a description of each of the six steps that make up HEARTS. The first sentence of each step corresponds to the same prompt in the reproducible teacher resource. Each of the classroom vignettes related in the book follows the HEARTS mindfulness-based teaching approach and can be easily cross-referenced. Of particular importance to the HEARTS approach is to apply the chosen mindfulness quality into the teaching context, and to do so intentionally. This intention is the thread that is interwoven into each of the six steps.

The final step, self-reflecting for self-renewal and self-transformation, is of prime importance. Self-reflection is sorely lacking in our busy workplaces, yet it is so vital. It can also be one of the hardest skills to grasp and put into practice. Here the spotlight is focused on introspection and self-examination. Self-reflection relates to oneself and to what has been learned about one's own growth. It begs articulation of new insights into the self: how one's heart was moved, how one's inner being was touched, how one's mindfulness quality was enhanced. This is the place where personal growth can be affirmed, an inner shift can be recognized, or an aspiration can be achieved. Ideally, such insights bring self-transformation at a visceral level: a seed of mindfulness taking on new life, nurturing mindfulness as a way of being and cultivating teaching from the heart of mindfulness.

The Mindfulness Quality

HEARTS, which follows a six-step process once a mindfulness quality has been defined, begins by first identifying the mindfulness quality that you want to more intentionally integrate into your life. Mindfulness qualities are ethical qualities that nourish a growing sense of wholeness, are universal in nature, and make us better human beings. You may have already been thinking about a mindfulness quality in different ways and in different areas of your life even before this first step. The HEARTS mindfulness-based teaching approach encourages the mindfulness quality that you have identified to be a primary focus in your teaching life. Mindfulness qualities that I have chosen for my own journey, qualities such as kindness, gratitude, and other ethical values I hope to integrate more into my life, are included in the book as examples to choose from but they are not all-inclusive. Qualities such as service, humility, and a host of others are equally valuable. I encourage you to think of areas of particular importance to you that nourish your practice, personalizing HEARTS to suit your own context and deepening your own journey into mindfulness.

The identification of a mindfulness quality can be inspired by your religious practice, your educational philosophy, or any source that is directly related to your own aspirations for the mindfulness qualities you wish to promote in your own life. Some practices may resonate more with who you are and others may be more challenging, but each time you take a step on the journey you come more into your authentic self, nourishing a sense of wholeness and well-being. Students appreciate this effort, and they can easily notice the difference between, on the one hand, a teacher who is in the process of becoming more and more mindful while implementing an activity and, on the other hand, a teacher who may do a fifteen-minute mindfulness activity but is still highly stressed throughout the school day.

The Six Steps

Heartfelt understanding of the mindfulness quality. Describe the mindfulness quality in your own words. Rather than finding a dictionary meaning or copying an explanation from a book, it is better to draw your understanding from a personal perspective, preferably one that springs from deep within your heart. A heartfelt relationship with the mindfulness quality taps a deeper inner wisdom. Thus, a more heartfelt mindfulness practice is imbued from the inception of the mindfulness-based teaching approach.

Explain the current classroom challenge. Write down a detailed description of the classroom challenge you are facing. Sometimes classroom challenges are glaringly obvious; at other times, it may seem like everything is going well and there are no issues that need particular attention. However, with careful analysis you will always be able to identify some student behavior or skill that can be improved and therefore considered a classroom challenge.

Apply the mindfulness quality intentionally. Apply a conscious decision-making process with deliberate awareness in order to integrate the mindfulness quality intentionally. This key step can be thought of as a paradigm shift—that is, until it becomes grounded in practice. The most important point is to integrate the mindfulness quality as part of the process, and do so intentionally. Applying the mindfulness quality intentionally connects the inner practice to the classroom challenge. This intention can be directed at you, the teacher, and the way you are approaching the situation, or it can be directed at the student and a behavior or quality you would like to see cultivated in the student. Initially the fit may have to be forced, but over time, this shift in perspective becomes seamless and automatic: it becomes a holistic, habitual understanding, rather than a step-by-step procedure.

Review the repertoire of classroom teaching strategies. Review and then choose one or more effective classroom teaching strategies from your own teaching repertoire. These may be time-tested techniques or perhaps a favorite classroom activity. Decide on a classroom teaching strategy that cultivates the mindfulness quality and meets the classroom challenge most effectively.

Take note of student learning. Take note and assess student learning after meeting the classroom challenge. A teacher's primary goal is to achieve positive results in student learning; therefore, it is important to clearly note and record student learning outcomes. These may be a very specific skill that the student acquired or may be an overall behavioral goal the student demonstrates. When the assessment of student learning is measurable, evidence of student progress can be clearly communicated.

Self-reflect for self-renewal and self-transformation. Self-reflect for teacher self-renewal and personal self-transformation. This important last step better ensures your own well-being is also being addressed, both professionally and personally. Moreover, taking time to reflect on how one's heart was moved, how one's inner being was touched, how one's mindfulness quality was enhanced, cultivates the mindfulness quality and nurtures teaching and living from the heart of mindfulness.

MINDFULNESS QUALITY
WHAT QUALITY OR ETHICAL VALUE DO I WANT TO CULTIVATE?

HEARTFELT UNDERSTANDING OF THE MINDFULNESS QUALITY.

HOW CAN I EXPLAIN THIS QUALITY IN MY OWN WORDS?

EXPLAIN THE CLASSROOM CHALLENGE.

WHAT IS THE CLASSROOM ISSUE I AM FACING?

APPLY THE MINDFULNESS QUALITY INTENTIONALLY.

HOW DO I INTEGRATE THE MINDFULNESS QUALITY IN WHAT I DO OR WHAT THE STUDENT DOES?

REVIEW AND IMPLEMENT APPROPRIATE CLASSROOM TEACHING STRATEGIES.

WHAT SPECIFIC TECHNIQUES, LEARNING STRATEGIES, OR ACTIVITIES WILL I IMPLEMENT?

TAKE NOTE OF STUDENT LEARNING.

WHAT WERE THE RESULTS IN STUDENT LEARNING?

SELF-REFLECT FOR SELF-RENEWAL AND SELF-TRANSFORMATION.

HOW HAS THIS MINDFULNESS QUALITY BEEN FURTHER CULTIVATED IN ME? HOW HAVE I CHANGED? WHAT ARE ANY NEXT STEPS?

HEARTS – A MINDFULNESS-BASED TEACHING APPROACH (MBTA)
© 2015 *Teaching from the Heart of Mindfulness* BY LAUREN ALDERFER
PUBLISHED BY GREEN WRITERS PRESS. DESIGN BY TRAVIS HELLSTROM.
THIS POSTER, WITH COPYRIGHT NOTICE, MAY BE COPIED FOR INSTRUCTIONAL USE.

MINDFULNESS PRAYER FLAGS

Mindfulness Prayer Flags are visual reminders to bring us back to the focus of attention. The prayer flags can be cut around the dotted lines, then hung individually, in a line, with the same message on each side, or individualized with your own message. Be creative and have fun!

CALLIGRAPHY DESIGNS BY LAUREN ALDERFER
©2015 *Teaching from the Heart of Mindfulness* BY LAUREN ALDERFER
THIS PAGE, WITH COPYRIGHT NOTICE, MAY BE COPIED FOR INSTRUCTIONAL USE.

Mindful BREATH Acrostic

*Mindfulness isn't difficult—we just
need to remember to do it.*

—SHARON SALZBERG

 Overview

THERE ARE A GROWING NUMBER OF RESOURCES
AVAILABLE TO TEACHERS who want to integrate a
mindfulness practice into their daily teaching lives.
Online courses, apps, blogs, conferences, college
courses, and training for teacher certification in
mindfulness are but a few examples. All aim to bring a
more focused, quieter mental space; this, in turn, slows
the breath, calms the heart, and brings more focus and
intention to each thought, word, and deed. Calming
activities such as walking quietly in the woods, laz-
ing in the sun at the shore's edge, snuggling up by

a warm fire on a cold winter's night are all conducive to encouraging stillness and cultivating mindfulness. A typical school day, however, may seem like the exact opposite: a bewildering variety of student levels and needs to be met, ever-increasing academic student goals to be achieved, unexpected interruptions, social media and IT-related concerns, security issues, the exigencies of school-related obligations beyond classroom teaching, to name just a few. The biggest challenge is to stay steady, grounded in mindfulness, in all this commotion.

Why not turn daily common occurrences into mindful moments throughout a busy teaching day? Daily school activities and routines can become seamless opportunities to slip into a mindfulness frame of mind and a mindfulness way of being, more and more, throughout the teaching day. Rather than imposing another activity or integrating a new technique, common occurrences throughout the school day can serve as chances to self-monitor the degree to which mindfulness is being observed, if it is being observed at all, or to bring mindfulness back into the moment.

The Mindful BREATH Acrostic, offered on the next spread, is based on my school setting. You may want to develop your own list of mindful acrostics, spelling out words that resonate better for you or including information that is better suited to your particular school context. You may want to make up a classroom acrostic together with your students or have students make up their own acrostics to guide their own mindful moments. Ideally, tools such as the mindful moment acrostic are integrated into a wider mindfulness-based approach to teaching. Developing such an approach to teaching creates a context in which mindfulness is the essential perspective. Then such tools better nurture mindfulness as a way of being, cultivating teaching from the heart of mindfulness.

B — BREATH

THE AVERAGE PERSON INHALES AND EXHALES 21,600 TIMES PER DAY. THE MORE STRESSED, THE FASTER THE BREATH. CONVERSELY, THE MORE TRANQUIL WE ARE, THE SLOWER AND DEEPER THE BREATH IS. SINCE MINDFULNESS IS CULTIVATED IN A FIELD OF TRANQUILITY, WE MAY WANT TO CHECK THE BREATH AND OBSERVE ITS PACE. EACH TIME WE INHALE AND EXHALE WE HAVE AN OPPORTUNITY TO CULTIVATE MINDFULNESS AND BECOME MORE PEACEFUL. ANCHOR BREATH, BELLY BREATH AND OTHER PRACTICES THAT HELP BRING AWARENESS TO EACH BREATH HELP SLOW DOWN THE BREATH AND WELCOME IN A MINDFUL MOMENT. SO WHENEVER YOU TAKE A BREATH, WATCH THE BREATH, SLOW DOWN THE BREATH. **OBSERVING THE BREATH NON-JUDGMENTALLY ENCOURAGES A MINDFUL MOMENT IN THE SCHOOL DAY.**

R — REMINDERS

SCHOOL BELLS, ANNOUNCEMENTS ON THE PA SYSTEM, THE CLOCK TICKING OR EVEN THE BEEP OF AN EMAIL ENTERING THE INBOX THROUGHOUT THE SCHOOL DAY MAY BE CONSIDERED ANNOYANCES. HOWEVER, AN APPARENT ANNOYANCE, SUCH AS A BEEP, CAN BE A REMINDER TO PRACTICE MINDFULNESS. THE BEEP CAN BE PROGRAMMED AS A MELODIOUS BELL. THERE ARE FREE IT APPLICATIONS THAT CAN PROGRAM DIFFERENT SOUNDS, SUCH AS A TIBETAN BELL, TO GO OFF AT DIFFERENT INTERVALS. UPON THE SOUND OF A SOOTHING SOUND BECOMES A REMINDER TO REMEMBER THE BREATH, OBSERVE ONESELF OR GAIN INSIGHT INTO A MINDFUL MOMENT. **REMINDERS ENCOURAGE A SPRINKLING OF MINDFUL MOMENTS THROUGHOUT THE SCHOOL DAY.**

E — EVERYDAY ROUTINES

STARTING WITH THE MOST FREQUENT ROUTINE SUCH AS LOOKING AT THE CLOCK ON THE WALL JUST BEFORE A CLASS BEGINS OR ENDS, A COMMON PRACTICE AMONG TEACHERS, IS A GOOD STARTING PLACE TO PRACTICE MINDFULNESS. ONCE ONE ROUTINE BECOMES A WAY TO PRACTICE MINDFULNESS, OTHER EVERYDAY ROUTINES IN THE CLASSROOM SEEM NATURAL: STANDING IN FRONT OF STUDENTS, GETTING UP AND DOWN FROM A CHAIR WHEN HELPING A STUDENT, OPENING OR CLOSING A BOOK, LAPTOP, OR OTHER IT DEVICE. THROUGHOUT THE SCHOOL FACILITY, SIMILAR EVERYDAY ROUTINES TO PRACTICE MINDFULNESS ABOUND: WALKING DOWN THE HALL, GOING TO THE RESTROOM OR OPENING OR CLOSING THE CLASSROOM DOOR AT THE BEGINNING AND END OF EACH DAY. **EVERYDAY ROUTINES BECOME INVITATIONS TO PRACTICE MINDFULNESS IN THE CLASSROOM AND BEYOND.**

A — AWARENESS

BUILDING AWARENESS IS A LIFELONG SKILL. AWARENESS INVITES SELF-OBSERVATION AND DEEPER INSIGHTS. THIS CAN BE BROUGHT TO THOUGHT, WORD AND DEED AND INTO EVERY TEACHING MOMENT. THE BREATH, REMINDERS THROUGHOUT THE SCHOOL DAY AND EVERYDAY ROUTINES ALSO OFFER OPPORTUNITIES TO CULTIVATE AWARENESS. **AWARENESS OF MINDFUL MOMENTS HAS POTENTIAL TO CULTIVATE MINDFULNESS IN A POSITIVE WAY.**

T — TALKING

WHEN STEPPING INTO CLASSROOMS WHERE THE TEACHER HAS A SOFT, CALM AND GENTLE TEACHING VOICE, THE SENSE OF CALM AND EASE IN THE CLASSROOM ARE PALPABLE. SPECIFIC ATTRIBUTES SUCH AS THE TONE OF VOICE AS WELL AS THE VOLUME AND SPEED OF TALKING CAN SERVE AS INDICATORS TO DETERMINE THE DEGREE OF CALMNESS. SINCE CALMNESS CULTIVATES MINDFULNESS, BECOMING AWARE OF HOW WE TALK CAN DETERMINE OUR OWN LEVEL OF CALMNESS. WE CAN MODERATE IF NEEDED AND OBSERVE TO WHAT DEGREE WE ARE PRACTICING MINDFULNESS. **TALKING BECOMES A MIRROR FOR SELF-REFLECTION AND OPPORTUNITIES FOR MINDFUL MOMENTS.**

H — HELP

SEEKING OUT COMMUNITY TO SUPPORT A PRACTICE IN MINDFULNESS CAN BE SHARED WITH A FELLOW TEACHER ATTEMPTING TO DO THE SAME, WITH A GROUP OF TEACHERS TAKING A COURSE IN MINDFULNESS OR EVEN WITH AN ENTIRE FACULTY AT A MINDFUL SCHOOL. WHETHER IN SCHOOL OR OUTSIDE OF THE SCHOOL VENUE, WHETHER A FAMILY MEMBER OR FRIEND, A SMALL GROUP OR LARGE, TO HAVE FELLOW TRAVELERS AND LIKE-MINDED COMPANIONS IS A GIFT, BUT AN ESSENTIAL GIFT TO SEEK OUT AND CHERISH. **HELP LENDS REFLECTION AND ENCOURAGEMENT THAT NOURISHES THE CONTINUING PRACTICE OF MINDFULNESS AND MORE MINDFUL MOMENTS.**

BREATH

© 2015 *Teaching from the Heart of Mindfulness* by LAUREN ALDERFER
PUBLISHED BY GREEN WRITERS PRESS. DESIGN BY TRAVIS HELLSTROM.
THIS POSTER, WITH COPYRIGHT NOTICE, MAY BE COPIED FOR INSTRUCTIONAL USE.

THE TIBETAN ENDLESS KNOT IS ONE OF THE EIGHT AUSPICIOUS SYMBOLS. THE VERSIONS INCLUDED IN THE BOOK HAVE HEARTS IN THEIR PATTERNS. CAN YOU FIND THE HEARTS? HOW MANY HEARTS CAN YOU FIND IN EACH ENDLESS KNOT?

RUDRAKSHAS ARE COMMONLY REFERRED TO AS BEADS. WHEN STRUNG TOGETHER THEY MAKE A MALA OR NECKLACE. THE RUDRAKSHA IS ACTUALLY A SEED, AND EACH ONE HAS A NUMBER OF FACETS OR SERRATIONS ON THE FACE, WHICH ARE CALLED MUKHIS OR MUKHAS. EACH LINE ON THE RUDRAKSHA SEPARATES EACH MUKHI. THE RUDRAKSHA IN EACH CHAPTER HAS THE CORRESPONDING NUMBER OF LINES OF THAT CHAPTER. CAN YOU FIND THE LINES? HOW MANY LINES ARE ON EACH RUDRAKSHA?

MINDFUL FUN

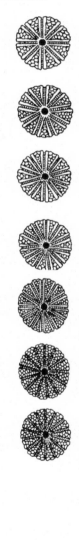

MINDFUL FUN
© 2015 *Teaching from the Heart of Mindfulness* BY LAUREN ALDERFER
THE TIBETAN SYMBOLS AND MOTIFS WERE USED WITH PERMISSION FROM
The Encyclopedia of Tibetan Symbols and Motifs @1999 ROBERT BEER, SHAMBHALA, BOSTON

❧ GRATITUDES ❧

ANY PEOPLE, known and unknown,
contribute to what is made manifest. A
myriad of causes and conditions, known
and unknown, are also part of the same contribution.
This book is just such an example. Coming to life
and being read by you, and hopefully touching your
heart, is the biggest gift of all, and for that I am most
grateful.

Thanks go out to all my students and the teachers
I have worked with over the years. Without them, this
book would never have been written. Daya and Sarah
have been both my students and wisest of teachers; I
thank them deeply.

To my Tibetan colleagues and friends in India,
whose humility I esteem and whose actions are so
worthy, I bow to you. Gaye Facer, Poonam Malhotra,

Shekhar Malhotra, Mary Kenny, Gene Parulis, and Sean Conley, thank you for bringing the first signs of life to this project.

To elevate an idea from its humble beginnings takes belief, expertise, vision, and heart. Thank you, Dede Cummings, for those gifts and for the elegance of the form. To Michael Fleming, whose editorial input raised the bar, creating a better experience for both the writer and reader.

To Travis Hellstrom, whose magic unfolds in this IT world that connects us all. Much appreciation to Audrey Batchelder, Molly Zapp, and the publishing and marketing teams, contributing their part to the greater whole. Gratitude goes out to Meena Srinivasan, Richard Brady, Parker J. Palmer, Tara Brach, and all the reviewers, connecting us through the heart of mindfulness.

My deepest, heartfelt, humblest of thanks to His Holiness The XIV Dalai Lama, whose inspiration, teachings, and living example have moved my heart and forever changed my life and karma.

The journey of this book has been one of my greatest teachers; as it traveled from the head to the heart, so did I. Henry—soulmate, steady companion, and teacher throughout the journey—my heart plunders mind of all its eloquence in gratitude to you.

Only from the heart can you touch the sky.

—RUMI

CPSIA information can be obtained at www.ICGtesting.com
Printed in the USA
BVOW08s0426220515

401370BV00001B/1/P